PARENTING for Character

Andrew Mullins

Using this book

Parenting for Character Applied is eminently practical. Here you will find a multitude of insights, case studies, points for reflection and practical exercises to work through on your own and as a couple, or with friends. You will focus on ways to improve your family life, and to raise your child to think clearly, choose wisely and love more deeply.

In the process you will discover a thousand ways to tweak your guidance, example, and family culture to be even more joyful and rewarding.

This book will help mum and dad work as a united team, on the same page. Talk about what you are seeing and thinking as you consider each topic. Talk deeply.

Set aside time weekly to fine tune your parenting. Schedule a walk, or chat over a glass of wine. But be committed. Start with the pages or topics that catch your eye, or simply begin at the beginning. The more united you are in your hearts and minds, the better your parenting will be. One page at a time.

There are also case studies and topics for you and your friends. This book can give structure to a monthly get together. But cap the formalities at 40 mins. Stay hungry.

These pages alone will not build character. But they will focus your parenting to be practical and tailored to the particular needs of your family. Your child will benefit, but you will also set goals for yourself. To do good we have to be good. Parenting skills must be reinforced and practised until they become second nature.

You will notice repeated points of emphasis. We will focus on building up the full range of good habits, on parent-child communication, on giving the right emotional example, on the wholly new demands of raising teenagers.

But all of this is at the service of teaching children to love wisely and well. And the surest way for you to teach children to love, is to show on your face all the joy that love brings into your life. This is the art of parenting.

All rights reserved ...

Copyright © 2023 by Parousia Media PTY LTD

All rights reserved. Except for quotations, no part of this book may be reproduced or transmitted in any form or by any means, electronic or mechanical, including photocopying, recording, uploading to the Internet, or by any information storage and retrieval system, without written permission from the publisher.

Published and Distributed by Parousia Media PTY LTD
PO Box 59 Galston, NSW 2159
Ph: +61 2 8776 8778
office@parousiamedia.com
www.ParousiaMedia.com

ISBN: 978-1-922968-72-2

Contents

Chapter 1
IS YOUR FAMILY A SCHOOL OF LOVE? — 5

Chapter 2
MAINTAINING UNITY — 25

Chapter 3
CLAIMING THE SPACE — 45

Chapter 4
FIX YOUR FACE — 65

Chapter 5
THE BUILDING BLOCKS OF CHARACTER — 85

Chapter 6
CARDINAL VIRTUES — 103

Chapter 7
SELF CONTROL — 117

Chapter 8
FORTITUDE — 137

Chapter 9
JUSTICE... GIVING OTHERS WHAT IS THEIRS BY RIGHT — 157

Chapter 10
SOUND JUDGEMENT — 179

Chapter 11
SELF-GIVING: THE TASK OF ADOLESCENCE — 201

APPENDICES — 225

Also by Andrew Mullins
Parenting for Character (2nd Edition, Parousia Media, 2020)
Parenting for Faith (Scepter Publishing, 2022)

Heart to Heart	Talk together Share from the heart Prioritise
Brainstorm	Brainstorm Reflect Set some goals Take the test
Parent–Child	Parent-child talk
Family Meeting	Family meeting Family activity
Discuss with Friends	Learning from others Discuss with friends Case study

Parenting for Character Applied is written to stand alone. Page references following each section, for example [P for C: 163], point to related material in *Parenting for Character (2nd edition)*.

Chapter 1

IS YOUR FAMILY A SCHOOL OF LOVE?

Your family is 'the place in which, more than anywhere else one learns to love. The family is a true school of love.'
Blessed Alvaro del Portillo

Talk together

Heart to Heart

Our core business is, by loving, to teach children to love. A friend was well and truly reminded of this priority by his three year old as was racing to get off to his work as a teacher one morning. He rushed back into the house to get something he had forgotten, and his little one stopped him and said, 'Kiss mummy, kiss the baby, kiss me, and then go to school.'

A parent's task is to lead their family to the heights of love. We are meant to live for others, utterly and off the charts. This is the core business of every family, to lead its members to be Einsteins, Federers, and Bradmans, in love. None of us may be geniuses but we can learn to love with everything we have got. Love is the key to the castle. Everything depends on this.

This book is designed to help you think through the quality of your parenting, the practical aspects of your parental love which will teach your child truly to live for God and others.

Love is always in the details – in a smile, warmth of affection, time to talk, encouragement, forgiveness and joyful service. When these things are missing, love has walked away. How is that possible? We can go without so many things in our homes, but not love.

Across the road from my house is an inner-city coffee window. There is practically no room in the shop so those sipping their brew tend to sit on the simple street benches. Recently when I walked past a little boy was telling his mum, 'I love you mummy'. 'I love you too', she replied. The power of the moment caught me by surprise. I was back with my own mum so many years ago.

How easy to miss the big target, and instead spend our days taxiing kids, working, shopping, cooking and washing, cleaning up, folding laundry! Integrate. Integrate. Integrate. We must integrate love into every activity, all things done at the service of love.

This is the great task of education. Pope Francis writes:

> 'No family drops down from heaven perfectly formed; families need constantly to grow and mature in the ability to love.'

This mission requires superior parenting skills.

Chapter 1

Children do not raise themselves. A child needs good habits in the four great domains of human action – in our habits of doing the things we enjoy, in our habits of doing difficult things for a good reason, in our dedication to those with whom we share our lives, and in the habitual way we think objectively, honestly, and practically. If not, feelings and impulses take over and we open the door to self-indulgence and self-righteousness and ultimately, frustration.

'The child is father of the man' wrote William Wordsworth. Our adult personalities are starting to form from our earliest years. We see many of the same traits in our personalities that were already on show in kindergarten - shyness or extroversion, boldness or holding back. But along with our temperament, we also see features that may have become more and more entrenched: kindness or thoughtlessness, bossiness or agreeableness. There will be many pleasant surprises, but for the most part our characters follow that hard-to-dodge law of character development: the best predictor of future performance is past performance. Make no mistake, what you do when your child is young makes all the difference to their happiness later.

    1.   What do we need to do to make our homes 'schools of love'?

    2.   What are the biggest obstacles to this?

[P for C: 163]

Start with the End in Mind

Heart to Heart

Share from the heart

*'"Cheshire Cat," she began, rather timidly... "would you tell me, please,
which way I ought to go from here?"
"That depends a good deal on where you want to get to," said the cat.'*
Lewis Carroll, *Alice in Wonderland*

Where do you want to get to in your family life and parenting? What is your goal? To keep your kids safe? To get them ready for adult life? What are your priorities? Is your home a school of love?

In each section below, tick the strategies most important in your unique family.

Resilience & self control
- Build resilience by helping children fight the little battles against pampering themselves with food, phones, fads and television.
- Help children put people above things.
- Model a positive attitude; avoid complaining and dwelling on criticisms.
- Teach the virtues of working hard, of physical toughness and endurance. Make light of tiredness and inconvenience.

Generosity
- Help children discover the duty we have to help others in need.
- Let children experience the happiness of family where we care for each other.
- Teach the link between generosity and happiness.
- Learn gratitude by example.

Good preparation for human relationships
- Prepare children for permanent relationships of love, by learning the difference between feelings and convictions, between impulses and deliberate decisions.
- Insist on loyalty and on taking full responsibility for all decisions that one makes.
- Raise with an understanding of the beauty of human love, sexual responsibility, and commitment.
- Invest much creativity in family life. Show that love means living for others.

Parenting itself is made up of good parenting habits. If parenting is the art of teaching children to love, then surely, in the process, parents perfect their own love. Love is more than feelings; it is the capacity to give of oneself to other persons, to live for others. In our hearts we know that our mission in life involves dedication to others but there is always a tension between this awareness and the self-focused individualism that our culture promotes.

What strike you as the most important parenting habits in which, as a couple, you wish to excel?

_____
_____
_____

[P for C: 86]

The Unique Strengths of Your Child

Prioritise

Heart to Heart

'Love, I would say, is that capacity which enables him to grasp the other human being in his very uniqueness.'
Victor E. Frankl

Separately from your spouse decide on five qualities and areas to develop in your child and then compare notes.

Strengths and areas to improve			
Mum		**Dad**	
Strengths I see in my son or daughter _____	Priority areas for development	Strengths I see in my son or daughter _____	Priority areas for development
1.			
2.			
3.			
4.			
5.			

P for C: 119]

Remove Those Rose Coloured Glasses

'Love me when I least deserve it, for that is when I really need it.'
Swedish proverb

Think if any of these common problems are touching your child's life. Find an example .

Challenge	Example
Sometimes not honest	
Can be wilful	
Can be disobedient	
Tends to run on feelings	
Easily distracted	
Preoccupied with own needs	
Does not look after things very well	
Not very orderly	
Impulsive	
Takes the comfortable chair	
Can be discouraged	
Easily bored. Lacking creativity	
Preoccupied with food	
Feels sorry for self	
Doesn't think ahead	
Has to be asked to help	
Finds it hard to share	
Doesn't often say thanks	
Could be more generous	
Answers back	
Seems easily led	

All these challenges are very normal, and so must be kept in perspective, but if they become patterns of behaviour that are entrenched in your child's character, there will be unnecessary roadblocks in your child's development.

If any of these challenges cause you to become impatient and cranky, you are missing a most important principle of parenting. Model the emotion you want to see. And remember that only love unites; resentment and self-serving emotion separate. Let us become experts at bringing children with us.

[P for C: 12]

Addressing the Needs of Your Child

Take the test

Consider your own child. In the columns to the right, prioritise these needs according to the need for you to change your current approach	Urgency to change		
	low	med	high
Safety			
1	Shelter			
2	Health ... sleep, healthy food.			
3	Clear limits and expectations. Receiving a 'No' when the physical or moral danger cannot justify the enjoyment or autonomy.			
Emotional needs			
4	To experience of the security and reassurance of family.			
5	To feel understood and listened to.			
6	To feel that their opinion is consulted in decisions that affect them, and that if you over-rule, that you explain why, simply with affection.			
7	Affection... in lots of different ways.			
8	Unconditional love. Show no negative emotion. No cold shoulders.			
9	That you provide example of a positive mindset and peaceful heart .			
10	That as much as possible you keep presenting the good true and beautiful in life, learning, entertainment, and culture, along with the evident joy that it gives you.			
11	Example of constant joyful engagement with people, especially with family members.			
Encouragement developing the habits and skills of adult life			
12	Practice in thinking for himself or herself.			
13	Practice in solving own problems.			
14	Practice in looking after others.			
15	Practice in setting own goals.			
16	Affectionate correction when a negative pattern develops and the help to set personal goals for improvement.			
Courage to improve the world			
17	Ideals.			
18	Practical know how to carry ideals into action.			
19	Experience of the joy that comes from helping others.			
20	Encouragement when actions require fortitude.			
21	Your example of courageously facing and addressing issues despite personal discomfort.			
22	Example of never passing by a person in need if we can do something to help.			

[P for C: 2]

Write a Family Mission Statement

Family Meeting

'... what could be compared to the forming of a soul and to helping the development of a young person's mind.'
St John Chrysostom

In preparation, Google some family mission statements. Go for the best. Print them out as samples. Hold a family meeting to write a family mission statement together. Here are some discussion starters:

- ☐ Do we want a joyful home? What will make our home joyful?
- ☐ What is the place of kindness in our home? Should we be kind all the time? Should we help each other whenever we need a hand?
- ☐ Should we help others outside our family? Will that help us to be happy?
- ☐ Are people more important than things in our home? When do we need to make a special effort?
- ☐ Are people more important than devices and screens in our home?
- ☐ Are we happier when we care for each other?
- ☐ Will it make me happy to be all the time watching what others do or have or wear?
- ☐ Do good times in our family need to be 'expensive' times?
- ☐ Are chores to help others? Or are they just jobs that have to be done?

Map out a mission statement for the best family in the business.
Give everyone a role in decorating the mission statement. Put it up prominently.
Review it together, initially weekly.

[P for C: 42]

Chapter 1

Trust is a Foundation

Case study

'Trusting no man as his friend, he could not recognize his enemy when the latter actually appeared.'
Nathaniel Hawthorne, *The Scarlet Letter*

> When our six-year-old daughter went next door to play with the little girl next door, the parent encouraged the girls to use make up. When our daughter said 'My parents don't want me to use make up yet', the neighbour said, 'This is a secret between you and me'. We were really upset when our daughter told us so we went straight over and calmly but clearly explained that we cannot have someone encouraging our daughter to keep secrets from us.

1. How would you have reacted?

2. How do you turn this into a win for all people, parents and children, involved?

[P for C: 134]

Building Family Traditions

Learning from others

'Have the courage to teach children austerity. If not, you won't accomplish anything.'
St Josemaria

Listed below are actual quotes from other parents. Be creative. Adapt some to your own purposes. Perhaps tick the ideas you really like. Be sure to note the goals you set yourselves.

Mealtimes

- We try to do things together. We all eat together including dad. We sit down for dinner together and encourage all to remain at the table until the last person finishes.
- There is lively discussion at mealtimes and on weekends - stories from the past – and no-one is allowed to interrupt another's story until finished.
- Everyone contributes to discussion at the dinner table. We have the custom, starting with the child who has finished first, to talk about 'What were the memorable moments today?' and afterwards 'What was the best/worst part of your day?' We also ask the kids to talk about their extra-curricular results (music and sport). When there has been a victory or a good mark, there are great accolades from all the family and a family treat.
- We try to ensure we eat breakfast together to start the day as a family.
- Sunday lunch is important whenever possible.
- The evening meal has more formalities.
- If there are too many interruptions to the person talking, we bring out the 'talking stick' which the person talking holds while the others listen attentively.

What are your goals, not your rules, for family mealtimes?
_____
_____
_____

Birthdays

- Celebrate birthdays of extended family as well.
- Children are the prince/princess for the day on their birthday.
- For birthdays we always have candlelit and special treats afterwards.
- Birthday celebrations are always with streamers, balloons, and a lot of fuss for the person on their day.
- We have a birthday procession.
- For the whole extended family, we hold a big birthday party once a year.
- We celebrate family members' birthdays or anniversaries with an extended family dinner and get-together.
- We tell stories about our child's birth and earliest years on his birthday.

How do you make birthday celebrations memorable in your family?

_____
_____
_____
_____

Family meetings

- We have family meetings occasionally on Sundays to discuss progress or challenges we are facing in the home.
- In our meetings each member has a chance to voice out their opinions concerning family issues.

How do you structure your family meetings?

_____
_____
_____
_____
_____

Family get-togethers

- We love extended family get-togethers with grandparents, aunts, uncles, etc. These are always very enjoyable and looked forward to by our children.
- We plan Friday night entertainment and supper afterwards.
- Monday is our Family Night. We have a special dinner followed by various family activities.
- Afternoon tea daily is the best time for discussion with all the children.
- We ask the children to save up awards and special news to surprise everyone at dinner time (they usually tell mum first so she can coordinate turns) also talking about interesting or annoying items. It is important to learn to plan ahead to share with everyone.
- We try to have a nightly laugh together. We try to bring a funny story to the table every day.
- We often have a family games night where the whole family can be involved. The little children join in to train i.e., Monopoly, Scattergories, Trivial Pursuit, etc.
- Every now and then we have a comedy night at home. It's so good for kids to see mum and dad being zany.
- We love spontaneous family outings which don't take a lot of planning.
- In the holidays we have a pyjama day where the family spend the day at home together doing enjoyable activities.

What do your children love about your family get-togethers?

_____
_____
_____
_____
_____

Family affection

- We ensure we each spend some one-on-one time with each child at some time during the week.
- We show we respect our children when we take time to stop and pay attention to what they have to say. And of course we encourage respect through the way we, the parents, speak to one another.
- We have moments for greeting and kissing: upon waking, before sleeping, arrival and leaving home and after Mass.
- Grandparents are an integral part of our family. In our culture children kiss the hands of grandparents as a sign of respect. We teach them to address other parents and our friends as Tito (uncle) and Tita (auntie) as a feature of respect.
- All our children are encouraged to greet grandparents, parents, and adult relatives with a kiss.
- We teach the children to telephone or write a note of thanks for presents received.
- We always wish each other well with a smile.
- In the kitchen we have a chart for smiley stamps against each child's name for kindness, extra effort, etc.
- Breakfast in bed made by the kids is a feature of every Mother's and Father's Day.
- Our adult children come home for family orientated special occasions, such as Christmas, and Easter, even when this involves interstate travel.
- We try at least every month to have a one on one time with each child (mum or dad with one child only), doing something they both like (shopping together or driving to the tip! We find this uninterrupted talk time is important to stay in touch with them individually. It is too easy to communicate collectively.
- On Holy Saturday we always hide Easter eggs about the house and garden.
- At Christmas time we have a sweep because of the large number of family members. Each adult buys for another adult and each adult has one or two children to buy gifts for, and it all stays very secret until Christmas Day.

What do you think your children will most vividly remember about the affection you show them?

_____
_____
_____

Activities together as a family

- We try to go out for dinner once per week, something different but not expensive, and we love camping holidays during school vacations.
- As a family we love physical activity: tennis, bikes, etc.
- We try to have a short annual holiday with family activities, fishing, swimming, walking.
- Our approach is good, well-planned, cheap family holidays.
- We go to the same area on the coast each year for annual holidays. The kids have become very familiar with this area of the country.

What do you think your children enjoy most about family time together?

_____
_____
_____

[P for C: 28, 148]

Sayings of Rafael Pich

Learning from others

'Say but little and say it well.'
Ancient wisdom

Read these tips from this global family educator, himself a father of sixteen.

Tick the sayings you like best for your own parenting.

- ☐ 'A strong family life is the answer to all the challenges that society can throw at us.'
- ☐ 'Raise children to solve their own problems in life.'
- ☐ 'We must grow every year for the benefit of our children. We should apply *professional* expertise to raising our children, studying how to be a better parent.'
- ☐ 'Kids have the right to speak alone with mum and dad.'
- ☐ 'Children have a right to make a mess in the kitchen and a right to clean it up after themselves.'
- ☐ 'All members of the family should normally be present at least at one meal every day.'
- ☐ 'We are in the age of monopolistic mums and absent dads.'
- ☐ 'A family alone is vulnerable.'
- ☐ 'It is wise for parents to become close friends of the parents of their children's friends.'
- ☐ 'The more we get to know others the more we love them.'
- ☐ 'You only give your children good food to eat, so what food for the brain and for the heart do you give your children?'
- ☐ 'Golden age of education... up to three years old; silver age...up to six; after six... stone age.'
- ☐ 'When something goes wrong, rejoice. We can now see and address the cause of a problem that before was hidden.'
- ☐ 'Work at home for children promotes the early maturity of children.'
- ☐ 'Children have the right to learn how to look after themselves.'

[P for C: 2]

Auditing Your Concerns

Share from the heart

Heart to Heart

Tick topics below that are also a significant concern for you and your spouse.

Parents of infants are most concerned about:
- ☐ Not sleeping
- ☐ SIDS
- ☐ How to react to crying baby
- ☐ Laying foundations for discipline
- ☐ Communicating well as a couple to share the load
- ☐ Emphasising motor and talking milestones

Parents of younger children are most concerned about:
- ☐ Frequent tantrums
- ☐ Children who do not obey
- ☐ Unmanageable sibling rivalry
- ☐ Children not being truthful
- ☐ Aggression and violence showing in behaviour
- ☐ Complaining and whining child
- ☐ Resistance to school
- ☐ Poor eating habits
- ☐ Addiction to gadgets
- ☐ Shyness and lack of confidence
- ☐ Overweight child
- ☐ Lack of friends

Parents of teens are most concerned about (according to a 2017 Mott Poll):
- ☐ Bullying/cyberbullying
- ☐ Children not getting enough exercise
- ☐ Unhealthy eating
- ☐ Internet safety
- ☐ Children falling into drug abuse
- ☐ Mental health
- ☐ Teenage pregnancy

You are not alone. There is a wealth of good material on the net to keep concerns in perspective and to follow best parenting practices. Now consider how the best parenting is proactive. What can you do during your child's pre-teen years to help avoid more entrenched teenage concerns? Formulate three clear strategies to respond to your greatest concerns.

1. _____

2. _____

3. _____

[P for C: 19]

Is There Depth of Kindness in Our Family?

Take the test

'Always think others better than yourself.'
Philippians 2:3

Justice comes down to treating others well habitually. All self-centred responses to others undermine this virtue. This virtue is best learned in a family where love is the overriding motivation.

Yet we can be blind to our own deficiencies, judging ourselves (and our children) on our own standards. Too easily we can teach children comply but without depth of kindness, mercy and empathy.

Talk as a couple. Do you ever fall into some of these categories?

- We easily run out of patience or get 'fed up'.
    - Parents need to try to model love that never runs out of patience and never gives up. Do we try to model habitual kindness? Are we open to feedback from each other?

- We are so busy our goal is to survive. The joy and love seem so distant.
    - Do I try to make service to my spouse and children the linchpin of family life? Do I give constant example of it?

- We seem to make the mistake of insisting on compliance with our instructions at the price of good manners and kindness.
    - Let's try not to become sticklers for order at the price of alienating spouse and children.

- We can be blind and accommodating to our own faults of self-indulgence and are reluctant to challenge our child in areas we are not demanding on ourselves.
    - We help each other with encouragement when we start to see in our children our own faults of eating too much, seeking out comfort, giving in to anger in our children.

- We want children to go at our pace when we are the ones who benefit. We can be selfish.
    - We each try to slow down, and be in the moment, going at the pace of our toddler when we are putting him to bed.

- We can find it hard to apologise and to admit our mistakes.
    - We expect children to be humble and secure in their relationships so we need to give better example.

[P for C: 25]

Audit Social Skills

Set some goals

Think of one action you can do to foster each of the following sentiments in your child?		Are there times when you notice the following behaviours in your child? Is there a pattern developing?	
Appreciation for others		Meanness	
Indebtedness to others		Entitledness	
Gratitude		Ingratitude	
Understanding for others		Lack of understanding	
Empathy		Carelessness	
Sensitivity		Insensitivity	
Admiration		Obliviousness to others' qualities	
Rapport		Poor social skills	
Compassion		Hard-heartedness	
Acknowledgement		Thanklessness	
Directness		Avoiding difficult discussions	
Simplicity		Overcomplicating things	
Capacity to apologise		Reluctance to apologise	
Cheerfulness		Negativity	
Light-heartedness		Preoccupation	

[P for C: 88]

And Love is Our Great Motivator

'Kids love what their parents love.'
Steve Ray

A family is the first place on earth where we should always do things out of love. We don't do things because we expect pocket money or a hug. We do things because we love the others. Full stop.

A family is the natural place therefore to learn the meaning of love from the example of the older family members.

A smile readily communicates love. We must make our own weather. Let us do our best to ensure that nothing takes away positivity and good humour. One of my most important tasks as a parent is to teach my child that happiness does not depend on events or other people.

- Am I mindful of the things that motivate me... my desires, feelings, passions, and drives?
- Do I notice that the things that give me joy, are often the things that give my children joy? If I crave pleasure, possessions, comfort, recognition, or affection... these will become also my children's key motivations because of my example.
- Do I self-manage gratifications: food, drink, comfort, available cash, play, delight in possessions, power, popularity?
- Are true choices underpinning my motivation, or do I find many of my motivations are impulses and habitual desires that may or may not be good for me?
- Do I teach that human beings have the power to choose what motivates us, not just allowing habitual desires and impulses to dominate our lives?
- Do I raise children to be intrinsically motivated? Or do they need external carrots, comforts, pleasures, bribes, money, as incentives?
- Do I use every opportunity to sow love between the members of my family, pointing out the good things that each one does, and emphasising the positive?
- Do I try always to lead by example, showing my delight in each family member?
- Do I strive never to keep tabs? Do I show my gratitude whenever I am helped?

[P for C: xii]

Think About the Core Parenting Skills You Need

Set some goals — Brainstorm

'Man cannot live without love. He remains a being that is incomprehensible for himself, his life is senseless, if love is not revealed to him, if he does not encounter love, if he does not experience it and make it his own, if he does not participate intimately in it.'
St John Paul II, *Redemptor Hominis*

ASSESS YOUR PARENTING QUALITIES	Level of Development					Priority areas
	Well developed	Fair to middling	Fair	Much work needed	Non-existing	
Unity between parents... in expectations, and in cooperation, and in frequent communication.						
Affection for each child independently of the child's good or bad behaviour.						
High but reasonable expectations.						
Readiness to give a good example in everything, at all times.						
Customs of close communication with each child Effective management of the influences coming into the lives of the children. Readiness to ensure that children accept the consequences of their mistakes and faults, provided they will not be harmed by these consequences.						
A high priority on honesty in your home, in your own behaviour and in your children's behaviour.						
Creativity in family life - a readiness to ensure that each weekend, from the time your children are young, you plan enjoyable family times together.						
Habitual cheerfulness that does not depend on external events, but rather on the peace of soul within you.						
A will to correct, with affection, but clearly and urgently.						
A determination to build good habits systematically in your children, presupposing a deep awareness of the needs of each child.						

[P for C: 36]

Identify Priorities in Your Approach to Building Character

Prioritise

Heart to Heart

Use this exercise to determine which strategies to prioritize in your own home. Invest a little time to get organised because priorities on paper are easier to manage.

Remember you are ranking yourselves, not your child.

Approach for developing character		1 (least) – 10 (well developed)									
		1	2	3	4	5	6	7	8	9	10
Training of more or less 'automatic' actions	Are you consistent in your expectations?										
	Do you focus on repetition to build habits?										
	For your child do you plan 'first experiences' that highlight the good, true and beautiful?										
	Do you calmly insist on obedience?										
	Do you delegate all that you can?										
	Do you show the joy that good actions bring?										
	Do you nurture kindness always in your child?										
	Are you affectionate and encouraging?										
	Do you correct your child's actions in matters that you have both prioritized?										
	Do you allow non-dangerous natural consequences of actions to run their course?										
Education of the mind	Do you teach a child to help out of love for the person they are helping?										
	Do you coach a child to purify their motives when selfishness creeps in?										
	Do you prioritise building intrinsic motivation over blind obedience?										
	Do you build habits of effortful attention in our child?										
	Are you explicit in teaching right and wrong?										
	Do you correct calmly and affectionately?										
	Have you established daily and weekly customs of trusting communication with each child?										
	Are you careful to screen out negative inputs and influences?										
	Do you coach your child to self-knowledge?										
	Are you united? Do you model the love you want to nurture?										

[P for C: 10]

Dream a Little

Share from the heart

Heart to Heart

'Dream no small dreams for they have no power to move the hearts of men.'
Johann Wolfgang von Goethe

This exercise helps you think about the great range of qualities of character needed in life but that we can often take for granted. It is a parent's role to lay the foundations for these qualities of character. Look over the long list of qualities below.

- a. Tick the qualities that already seem well developed in your child.
- b. Asterisk four or five others in each of the four columns that you most want to develop in your child's character.
- c. After you have worked through the list you might like to compare notes with your better half.
- d. Can you spot the common characteristics for the behaviours in each column... each column lists virtues that are part of one of the cardinal virtues: prudence, justice, fortitude and temperance.

• Grounded in reality. Does not live with unrealistic expectations, or false grasp of situations or abilities.	• Obeys willingly and promptly.	• Determined and courageous in face of difficulties.	• Has integrity and purity of heart.
• Loves truth.	• Attentive and good listener.	• Calm. Not prone to anger.	• Possesses self control with respect to food.
• Sincere with self.	• Empathetic and considerate.	• Patient.	• Possessing self control with respect to temper.
• Wants to know the right thing to do when not sure.	• A good friend.	• Resilient.	• Able to control curiosity.
• Has strongly held convictions about matters that are important.	• Reads social cues.	• Orderly.	• Enthusiastic in doing good for others.
• Is flexible about opinionable matters.	• Understanding. Adapts to various personalities.	• Persevering and persistent.	• Joyful and light hearted.
• Has deeply held ideals about what is true and good.	• Kind.	• Ambitious to be better.	• Serene and mild.
• Open minded, and able to listen, respect, and evaluate other opinions.	• Grateful.	• Courageous.	• Gentle.
• Wise. Able to reason to make independent free choices.	• Forgiving.	• Implements a growth mindset.	• Moderate. Does not need excess for enjoyment.
• Decisive and practical.	• Loyal and faithful.	• Conscientious.	• Exhibits self mastery.
• Reflective and able to think critically.	• Fair.	• Gives leadership when it will help others.	• Capable of wonder and awe.
• Naturally confident and optimistic.	• Cooperative and easy to work with. Good in a team.	• Forthright and unafraid to speak up.	• Detached from material things and from comforts, for a good reason.
	• Compassionate	• Capable of heroic self sacrifice for others.	• Detached from own opinions.
	• Merciful.	• Honours commitments	• Able to go without preferences without complaining.
	• Able to take full responsibility for actions.	• Able to ask for assistance when needed.	• Self controlled.
	• Values people more than things.	• Industrious and professional.	• Modest.
	• Sincere with others.	• Uses time well.	• Appreciates beauty.
	• Generous and loves wholeheartedly.	• Audacious in doing good.	

• Readily discerns truth from falsehood. • Mindful. Able to reflect on own feelings, dispositions and the situation. • Trustworthy. • Creative. • Humble. An absence of airs and self importance. • Committed to learning. • Able to set goals and prioritise.	• Generous and loves wholeheartedly. • Shows solidarity with those less fortunate. • Caring. • Appreciates how much we owe to others. • Deep sense of responsibility. • Tolerant. Accepting and respectful of persons. • Diligent. • Patriotic. • Thoughtful of how actions affect others.	• Honourable. Faces duty and wants to fulfil it. • Wants to develop the full range of talents. • Magnanimous. Seeks to bring to fruition great projects. • Daring. • Able to go without. • Ambitious to do good in society. • Looks on work as service. • Commits to timetables and jobs.	• Seeks all that is good, true and beautiful. • Light hearted. Able to see the humour in events and situations. • Able to say 'no' to self. • Carries self with deep peace of heart. • Detached from gadgets. • Able to avoid scattered attention.

[P for C: ix]

Chapter 2

MAINTAINING UNITY

'I try to remember that we each bring skills to parenting. It helps me to stay very united.'
One dad

Discuss with friends

My first day of teaching was rather memorable in various ways. I had been posted to a school in Sydney's west. In the principal's induction talk there was one sentence I have never forgotten: 'One thing you must realise is that everything you do here is conditioned by the fact that 80% of our families are in crisis. That colours everything.'

When families are in crisis, kids are the big losers. When parents are preoccupied with their own problems, kids go to seed. In 2021 Australian police dealt with over 6000 domestic and family violence matters a week. That's one every two minutes. Even before the pandemic, the number was increasing 4-5% per year each year. Too much anger. Too much hurt.

The unity of parents and their mutual love is the child's crucial first experience of human love, and where an intuition of God's love is grasped. In their families, children learn to relate to others, and to give of themselves.

Maintaining unity brings challenges. The building blocks of unity include attention, affection, listening, asking advice, constant service and doing things together. A friend writes from overseas, 'Unity with your wife is not easy. It is easy to get out of step and it is a feature of the relationship that needs constant attention. Our trip away has helped us a lot.' Some research appears to demonstrate that time together is proportionate, statistically speaking, to the very success of the marriage. David Isaacs, author of *Character Building*, insists on the value of 'doing things together', and of 'creating shared memories' of holidays and home decoration. 'Put up photos of the good times... they will give you hope, easing the way through every relationship's difficulties.'

Isaacs talks of the importance of total buy-in from both mum and dad for their great shared project as parents, not leaving the heavy family lifting to the other partner. Talk daily about the children. Adopt a parenting style does not just react to crises, but that builds character by consistent close follow up by parents.

One young mum explains that 'When I was pregnant and my husband arrived home after work, I just wanted to talk, but his attitude was "What is there to talk about?"' Agreed strategies are needed. One couple have this approach: 'To stay united with my wife, sometimes we say: "Let's start this conversation again". We try to understand the issues from each other's perspective.'

Unresolved issues are a timebomb. No topics can be taboo... money or bedroom issues, whatever is causing grief. There can be no topics off limits with one or the other shutting down dialogue. If this should happen much affection and prayer are needed, and then courage to address the issue. Sometimes men particularly need to move 'from facts to feelings' as Simon Carrington says in his couples talks: talking about their own feelings, and appreciating the feelings of their wife. One dad summed up the great benefits of unity in his family: 'When Sally and I are good, the kids are good.'

Discuss with friends.

1. What do we find are the hardest challenges to being united?
2. What have we discovered helps us to stay united?

[P for C: 4]

Weekly Team Meeting

Prioritise

Heart to Heart

'Do first things first, and second things not at all.'
Peter Drucker

1. Every week, perhaps over a glass of wine after the kids are in bed on the last Sunday night of the month, review the goal for each child, adjust it or tweak the support you give to child to achieve it. Reflect on your own efforts: are you giving enough encouragement? Is it specific enough? Is it the most suitable goal at this moment?
2. Have a simple clear current focus for each child's character... the more concrete the better: not to complain, tidy room each day before leaving, looking after little brother, trying again, sticking to one's personal afternoon schedule, not having to be asked twice, etc.
3. Decide who encourages the child the next day with the changes.
4. Both give ongoing encouragement during the week. Make sure there are reminders, guided assistance, recognition and positive reinforcement.

[P for C: 162]

Your Complementary Roles

Set some goals

How much good flows on to the family when mums and dads are united with resilient habits of communication helping them be of one heart and soul in their understanding of each other's limitations, and all the while complementing each other with their own strengths.

Which boxes can you tick. Then share your results.

Dad

- ☐ I deeply value my wife's work. I understand the pressures on my wife. I recognize and work with my wife's strengths.
- ☐ I understand the whole situation at home and I don't jump to conclusions.
- ☐ I am careful never to leave my wife unsupported in family matters. Each day I check in with my wife during the day to offer ongoing support. I know how to listen.
- ☐ I am aware of the moments when I need to help. I am present habitually at family meals.
- ☐ I give leadership in the home, ensuring we have a clear game plan for each child's character development.
- ☐ I don't talk down to anyone. I teach that charity is the most important virtue.
- ☐ I bring idealistic topics to the table. I am practical, positive and optimistic.
- ☐ With each child there is dedicated personal attention and generous time weekly.
- ☐ We try to work together on issues as a team. I strive to complement my wife's strengths.
- ☐ I teach children to have an unqualified respect for their mother.
- ☐ I am proactive in discussing human love in appropriate and ongoing ways with each child.
- ☐ For my son I am conscious that I am the image of what it means to be a man.
- ☐ I am an expert at showing affection to each member of my family in the way they like it.
- ☐ I try to give children the right degree of independence, neither too protective nor careless of their physical or moral welfare.

Mum

- ☐ I know how to let go and let my children take control of their own lives.
- ☐ I know how to let go of issues and play to the strengths of my husband.
- ☐ I teach responsibility to each child. I often reassess each child's abilities and extend limits.
- ☐ I try to give children the right degree of independence, neither too protective nor careless of their physical or moral welfare.
- ☐ I visualize the adult I want each child to become.
- ☐ I teach relationship skills, understanding, empathy and compassion.
- ☐ I never give people the cold shoulder.
- ☐ I am understanding and affectionate with my husband.
- ☐ I work with my husband's strengths.
- ☐ I raise the esteem of my husband in the eyes of our children.
- ☐ I am careful not to allow children to become fussy or self-indulgent.
- ☐ I avoid letting children grow up at the mercy of fads and fashions.
- ☐ I keep my sense of humour.
- ☐ By talking things over together I keep perspective on issues, even emotional issues.
- ☐ I try to lead by example in my efforts to be the best wife and mother.

[P for C: 18]

Real Empathy in Marriage

Share from the heart

Heart to Heart

'Selfishness is not living your life as you wish, it is asking others to live their lives as you wish.'
Oscar Wilde

Go through this table together. Ask your spouse to be honest with you about how he or she feels. Listen to each other. Understand what your spouse is saying. This is not about finding fault but of understanding and addressing the needs of one's spouse.

How well have you understood your spouse's concerns? With deep care not to bruise each other's feelings, ask each other about the concerns that you had not expected to hear. Don't defend yourself... listen and learn.

Do you ever feel this way?

Do you ever feel this way?	Explanation for what is happening.	What can the spouse do?	An action plan.	
			Husband	Wife
I'm not appreciated	Emerson Eggerichs finds that these are the two greatest fears that disrupt marriage relationships: the woman is most prone to feelings of being under appreciated, and the man, to not being respected. Eggerichs insists that physical affection and interpersonal attention are essential ingredients of the married relationship.	Initiate the physical affection that your spouse seeks.		
I'm not respected		Pay more attention. Look at each other. Value the things your spouse does.		
I'm not lovable	Shaunti Feldhahn's research suggests a variation on the above, that the predominant insecurities for spouses are: many women return to the fear that 'I'm no longer lovable', and men to 'I just can't measure up, my performance as a husband and father is inadequate.' Feldhahn suggests that spouses must think the best of each other. We cannot take each other for granted.	Husbands should affirm much more their commitment of love in words and affection.		
I'm not good enough		Spouses need to hear the words 'thank you' very much more often for the actions they do carry out.		

I'm not getting the support I need.	Particular temperaments can allow anxieties to become predominant and even obsessive.	A problem shared is a problem halved. Strategies for better communication, especially in times of parenting stress, help.		
I'm worried about money, the future, about having another baby, etc.				
I feel my spouse is too distracted from the family.	These reactions have in common a negative mindset that has been allowed to develop towards one's spouse.	Realise that differing temperaments can react differently to criticism, and that we all have slightly differently calibrated priorities. Compare notes. Develop the habit of speaking without rancour when there is an issue. Be open to feedback from your spouse.		
I can't put up with this person.				
I find it hard to forgive.	These are the fundamental attitudes of humility that underpin successful relationships	Virtues are acquired by repetition. Practice in small ways. Note the triggers that hinder, and the habitual courtesies that can assist, the response.		
I find it hard to apologise.				
I am distracted from what I know I should be doing.	This challenge does not focus on fears but rather on habituation to pleasures and distractions. In the moment the feeling of attraction to a distraction trumps all other reasons.	Practical strategies of attention to priorities help: a personal daily and weekly plan, and weekly agreement on priorities. Once convictions are rectified, it is matter of establishing pathways of behaviour that become, over time, more predominant.		
I bring baggage into the marriage that affects me and the relationship.	This baggage may have a temperamental component (eg domineering) but will always have a behavioural aspect (gambling, pornography, OCD, etc)	Usually some professional intervention can assist with practical strategies.		

Do you notice how important are the feelings and emotional reactions of each of you? A two-way solution is needed: genuine care of the other person, and better management of our own emotional reactions.

Real empathy tries not to judge but to support. This table can help us see our own insensitivities but also moments where we need to better manage our feelings lest our feelings can end up managing us. They can either lead us to feel unsupported or failing, or they can lead us to dismiss the feelings of the person we love most in this life. Feelings enrich and give us great joy, but negative feelings go rogue by causing anxiety and fear. Even positive feelings can go rogue by distracting us into self-centred escapes.

Set yourself a goal that will help you be a more supportive husband or wife. Formulate a clear resolution. Make whatever changes are needed to take your marriage to a Triple A+ level.

[P for C: 74]

Politeness Measures Respect

Politeness should communicate the depth of respect we have for others. It should never be reduced to a superficial and external social convention.

If you are brave, ask your spouse to grade you, and don't just accept the feedback, be grateful.

		/10 The higher the score the better.		
1.	I am approachable and have a welcoming face.	never	1 to 10	always
2.	I am positive and I give compliments.	never	1 to 10	always
3.	I am a good listener.	never	1 to 10	always
4.	I use a handkerchief when I cough or sneeze.	never	1 to 10	always
5.	I'm careful not to dominate conversations.	never	1 to 10	always
6.	I give others sufficient personal space.	never	1 to 10	always
7.	I reply to all messages immediately.	never	1 to 10	always
8.	I dress appropriately.	never	1 to 10	always
9.	I use my mobile at the table.	always	1 to 10	never
10.	I allow my mobile to interrupt conversations.	always	1 to 10	never
11.	I keep people waiting.	always	1 to 10	never
12.	I'm a complainer.	always	1 to 10	never
13.	I talk when I have food in my mouth.	always	1 to 10	never
14.	I gossip.	always	1 to 10	never
15	I use rough or crude language.	always	1 to 10	never
	Total			

A mark of >100 means you are on the right track.

Now discuss how you are passing on these life skills to your child.

[P for C: 15]

How Well do You Communicate?

Share from the heart

Heart to Heart

Answer these questions separately and compare notes afterwards.

- a. When do you both talk most easily?
- b. Do you find there is enough time to share in the day and in your week?
  - What do you think could help?
  - What topics cause arguments?
  - Do you ever quarrel in front of the children?
  - How do you stop arguments before things are said that hurt and wound?
- c. Do you feel you are united on all the big issues?
  - Money
  - Bedroom
  - Expectations of the children and family timetable
- d. Do you ever feel that you cannot raise some issues?
- e. Do you ever feel shut down in discussion?
- f. Are there topics which you don't like being discussed?
- g. When do you find it difficult to talk, be listened to, or be understood? Are you able to raise any matter in discussion without it leading to an argument?

Doing things together
- h. Do we enjoy doing things together?
- i. Are we aware of not doing things now that we used to enjoy together?

Teamwork
- j. Do we talk every day about the children, and at least each week in depth about each child individually?
- k. Do we talk about parenting?
- l. Do we give each other feedback freely?
- m. Do these conversations lead to practical resolutions for us both?
- n. Do we offer feedback that is objective and constructive?
- o. Is feedback ever negative or resentful?
- p. Do we agree on the priorities for each child's character development?
- q. Do we feel we agree in all parenting issues?
- r. Does our child look for a 'second opinion' from my spouse and does this cause problems?
- s. Does either of us ever feel undermined?

Consider yourself.
- t. Do I consider myself most grateful, most fortunate, and unworthy of so much love?
- u. Do I think often of my spouse's qualities?
- v. Do I love my spouse as a 'package' deal?
- w. Am I judgemental and fixated on particular behaviours?
- x. Am I blocking and defensive if I am criticized?

[P for C: 5]

Scenarios in Parental Teamwork

Case study

'If your marriage is a loving one you will provide a role model which your children will reach for when they grow up.'
Aaron Haas, *The gift of Fatherhood*

Teamwork is powerful. Mums and dads together form a great team, but each brings specific strengths, and each needs to bounce ideas off the other to moderate their reactions.

These case studies are particularly suitable for discussion suppers. Read the scenario, gather your thoughts and compare notes.

1. The family is eating dinner. Dad makes a comment critical of the food, or mum draws sarcastic attention to dad's late arrival. How can the parent who did not make the comment deal with this?
2. If your wife rings you at work about something she is not coping well with, how do you handle this?
3. A child is showing disrespect to his mother... what are the possible causes? How should you handle this?
4. After you very gently ask your fourteen year old son not to walk mud onto the lounge room carpet, he shouts, 'All you ever do is nag!' When does nagging work? When does it not work?
5. A child complains that dad doesn't have to make his bed or do the washing up. What does mum do?
6. What does dad do when his child shouts at mum, 'You never listen. It's not like that at all.'
7. 'Mr Hardn'asty has it in for me at school. He always picks on me. He said I was too untidy.' What are you going to say to your son?
8. Your daughter comes home from school and launches into tirade, 'I can't stand Maybelle. She such a Karen. She is always dobbing. I was kept in because of her.' How do you handle this?

It's not so much a question of exploring the specific incident in detail. Talk so that you are on the same page and you build skills to be proactive, to put principles of teamwork in place, or be better able to deal with different points of view in the future.

[P for C: 18]

Parental Leadership

'My father never had to be tough on me because he was so tough on himself.'
St John Paul II

Here is a wonderful story from Arrian's *Life of Alexander the Great*.

Alexander the Great was leading his army across a desert. All were tormented by thirst. Some scouts found a wretched little trickle in a shallow gully. They scooped up what they could in a helmet and hurried back to Alexander with their priceless treasure. With a word of thanks for the gift, Alexander took the helmet and, in full view of the troops, poured the water on the ground. Arrian says 'so extraordinary was the effect of this action that the water wasted by Alexander was as good as a drink for every man in the army... it was proof, if anything was, not only of his powers of endurance, but also of his genius for leadership.'

> *Arrian (1958), Life of Alexander the Great (Trans. Aubrey de Selincourt), Penguin: Harmondsworth, UK, p. 218.*

How can you apply this in your parenting?

[P for C: 36]

Sharpen the Saw, Generously

Reflect

Dad was up early on Mother's Day in the kitchen, 'Dad what are you doing?' Rather pleased with himself Dad replied, 'I'm cooking breakfast for mum. It's Mother's Day!' And his son replied spontaneously, 'Dad, does that mean every other day is Father's Day?'

1. What do you do to stay at your best? Stephen Covey's seventh habit of highly effective people is 'Sharpen the saw'- to perform at your best you need to stay sharp. For mum and dad that means be aware of each other's needs and looking after each other. The key is to think more of each other person than of oneself.
2. Consider core issues of intimacy, trust, total security, companionship, understanding, spiritual support, never feeling judged or manipulated, feeling unconditionally respected. Consider your spouse's needs according to the matrix below and whether you try to anticipate them. Don't paddle around in shallow platitudes,

	Physical needs	Social/emotional needs	Mental needs	Spiritual needs
Mum				
Dad				

3. Now tackle the same exercise for your child or children.

	Physical needs	Social/emotional needs	Mental needs	Spiritual needs

4. Addressing needs is but the first way of deeply caring for someone, but it is an essential way.

[P for C: 37]

Stress Testing Relationships

Share from the heart

Heart to Heart

'Why do you look so sad?'
'Because you speak to me in words, and I look at you with feelings.'
Tolstoy

Work to understand each other's concerns. Some of the greatest pressures on families are listed below. Read them together and talk about any of these that impact on your home and your habitual joy.

1. Financial stresses.
2. Time pressures. Parents busier than ever outside the home. Erosion of family life and family time.
3. Our own anxiety and stress, and loss of joy.
4. Emotional challenges to the extent that I feel unsupported or not understood.
5. A need for the broader emotional control which is at the very heart of virtue.
6. We fall into conflict too often. We don't seem to look at problems in the same way.
7. We know that happiness is in loving things not people but material things in our home cause conflict. We seem to be conditioning our children to comforts and having their whims addressed immediately. There is more and more pressure on us to buy more and more: toys, collectibles, clothes, and the latest fads and gadgets.
8. We are not good at handling children who are uncooperative or complaining.
9. Media and screen intrude into our family life.
10. We have serious safety concerns in area where we live, and when the kids are travelling.
11. We find our spiritual and ethical priorities are constantly being undermined by the state itself.
12. We feel undercut by other influences on their children such as peer group, social media, etc.
13. One of us particularly has difficulty in connecting with one of our children.
14. We have older children giving poor example.
15. To tell the truth we have lost a little hope that parents can do a magnificent job with their children.
16. We are not united in our approach: one of us is too stressed and concerned; or, one of us is not connecting with our child; or, one of us is just not in the game; or, ...

Keep this list on the table for a follow discussion in a few day's time.

[P for C: 152]

Dad's Deepest Wants and Desires

Reflect

'The three inspiring forces of nature are typhoon, earthquake, and father.'
Japanese saying

We need a spirit of self-examination. Often our desires can tell more about us than our actual behaviours.

- ☐ Do you maintain an active battle against the faces of self-centredness:
    - ☐ Self-indulgence (just one more drink)
    - ☐ Self-affirmation (talking about myself)
    - ☐ Self-justification (preferring my own opinion, having the last word)
    - ☐ Self-pity (holding grudges)
- ☐ Do you strive not to overplay your hand, not to be a dominating dad?
- ☐ How is your determination to live for your wife? So, do you strive to change yourself for your wife, to be more considerate, to be more attentive, to be more in love each day?
- ☐ Do you put address issues with urgency that are causing your wife concern and stress... can she leave things in your hands without reminders?
- ☐ How is the war against laziness in your life... doing the things you don't care much for (repairs, fixing taps, scrubbing walls, touching up walls, putting things away, gardening, etc).
- ☐ Do you teach your child that work is, above all, service to others?
- ☐ Do you keep your wife and family constantly in your thoughts ... what is making them happy and sad?
- ☐ Every night when you get home do you seek to know what have been the 'big' moments in the lives of each family member during the day?
- ☐ Do you pray insistently for your wife and each of your children?

[P for C: 121]

How High Are You Setting the Bar?

'The world will pass away, but love and music will endure.'
Gaelic proverb

To get to our final goal it helps to think of intermediate steps. This goal setting exercise below can help.

What do you see as the endpoints, the goals, to which you aspire in your parenting? How high are you setting the bar?

	Is this important to you?	✔ or ✗
1.	At least not forgetting a birthday or anniversary	
2.	Doing things together as a couple each week.	
3.	Finding weekly time to talking together as a couple about each child.	
4.	Weekly minimum one on one chats with each child	
5.	Planning together some creativity in family life every week.	
6.	Apologising whenever you have slightest reason.	
7.	Sharing the joys and sorrows of your spouse every night.	
8.	Letting each other know always where you are.	
9.	Deciding together about any extraordinary expense of note.	
10	Ringing if you are going to be late.	

This task can illustrate for us that at times we have mediocre expectations for ourselves.

[P for C: 97]

Am I Easy to Live With?

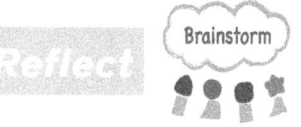

'When you are alone guard your thoughts, and when in your family, guard your temper.'
Matt Talbot

Can you tick these 20 boxes?

- ☐ Does my face light up when I see my children or my spouse after a long day? Do I greet everyone with a smile? Do I realise that I am responsible to create the emotional tone in my home by means of my face, my tone of voice and my body language?
- ☐ Am I optimistic?
- ☐ Am I good humoured? Do I make light of difficulties? Do I keep calm in the face of difficulties?
- ☐ Does it take a lot to upset me? Or am I an impatient person, or a person prone to crankiness or anger?
- ☐ Do I show my love by doing things without being asked?
- ☐ Do I put initiative into family activities?
- ☐ Am I even keeled? Or do I cause others to walk on eggshells?
- ☐ Do I say even difficult things in the kindest possible way, or am I prone to harsh or sharp comments?
- ☐ Am I quick to apologise, because sincere apologies are a prerequisite to fix inevitable offences. Do I model this life skill?
- ☐ Am I quick to forgive? Forgiveness is necessary to mend relationships.
- ☐ Do I make light of other's failings, or do I draw attention to them?
- ☐ Do I avoid criticising others who are not present?
- ☐ Do I nag my children and show my impatience? Do I model this life skill?
- ☐ Do I avoid moodiness or giving others the cold shoulder?
- ☐ Do I avoid complaining, or feeling sorry for myself?
- ☐ Do I put my clothes away? Do I put things back where they belong? Or do I leave things around?
- ☐ Do I avoid leaving dirty cups and dishes for someone else to clean?
- ☐ Do I clean up the bathroom after myself?
- ☐ Am I quick to do jobs when I am asked?
- ☐ Am I habitually on time?

Now be brave, share the results with your spouse and listen to each other's observations without being defensive.

[P for C: 163]

Backing Up Mum in the Home

'(Women are) sentinels of the invisible.'
St John Paul II

Invite some friends over for a discussion supper.

Part I. What are the biggest challenges mums face in their efforts to build human virtues in their children?

> *Brainstorm for ten minutes: List as many problems that members of the group can think of... then vote on the most important five or arrive at your selection through consensus.*

Try to ensure that the responses are wide ranging, coming from both mums and dads... the focus is on the objective challenges mums face.

Part II. For the agreed five biggest challenges, try to reach consensus on the most important things dad can do to help.

Cap the formalities below at one hour, then enjoy a relaxed chat.

[P for C: 81]

Practical Consistency

'From the beginning it was our house, so the kids knew they were expected to pull their weight in helping to maintain it.... Start young.'
Ray Guarendi, Back to the Family

Some challenges demand a united approach from parents.

The recommended total screen time for ages 0-2 is zero screen exposure; for ages 2-5, not more than one hour per day; for ages 5-17, no more than two hours recreational sedentary screen time daily. (https://www.health.act.gov.au/about-our-health-system/healthy-living/kids-play-active-play/screen-time/recommended-screen-time)

How do you and your spouse ensure you are united this?

1. Avoiding media and screen intrusion into family life.

   _____

2. Avoiding excessive screen exposure in a young child.

   _____

3. Raising children to have deep solidarity with the less privileged.

   _____

4. Raising children to have well chosen friendships

   _____

5. Raising children with ideals and faith.

   _____

[P for C: 21]

How Well Do You Support Your Spouse?

Share from the heart

Heart to Heart

Bill was walking behind his wife who was struggling in with the shopping from the car. With some difficulty the screen door was negotiated and multiple plastic bags deposited in the kitchen.
'Why didn't you help me?'
'You looked like you were coping.'

How can both husband and wife be more understanding and supportive? Considering your own efforts; don't find fault with your partner. This exercise is in three parts. Do this exercise separately. Then compare your thinking.

How well do you understand each other's fears? Tick beside statements that you feel are true for yourself or your spouse. Do this exercise separately without seeing each other's answers.

	Do you ever feel this way in your relationship	Do you think your spouse ever feels this way?
I'm not appreciated.		
I'm not respected.		
I'm not lovable.		
I'm not good enough.		
I'm not getting the support I need.		
I'm worried about money, the future, another baby, etc.		
I'm annoyed because my spouse is too distracted from the family.		
I can't put up with this person.		
I find it hard to forgive.		
I find it hard to apologise.		
I get distracted from what I should be doing.		
I bring baggage into the marriage that affects me and the relationship.		

Now compare notes... how well have you understood your partner's concerns? Remember this is not about finding fault but about understanding what your spouse is thinking.

[P for C: 163]

Preparing for Loving Fidelity

Share from the heart

Heart to Heart

'The family is the first place where we learn to love.'
Pope Francis

In our home how are we teaching the following?

• How important it is that those in love are united in heart and mind. How easily tension arises when expectations differ, and there is little empathy.	
• Open and trusting communication is an important quality in strong relationships. Cold shoulders don't work.	
• Discourtesy and contempt are destructive. We must hold our tongues when we are upset. Hurtful words stay in the memory.	
• Trust is essential but it can be eroded by putting personal and perhaps professional goals above the welfare of another.	
• It is not easy to make a clear-headed choice of one's partner for life if one is already committed sexually to the relationship. Genuine affection seeks the good of another and does not cloud one's judgement.	
• We need to forearm our child against toxins in relationships such as jealousy, infidelity, lack of empathy, lack of reliability.	
• It is difficult to recognise personality disorders such as narcissism or a tendency to manipulate others if one's choices are based on superficial aspects of character.	

[P for C: 14]

Love Mustn't Run Out

'Most adolescent problems can be alleviated or rectified by correcting tensions in the parent child relationship.'
Ross Campbell, *How to Really Love your Teenager*

What torpedoes parent-teenager affection?

How much mischief follows when a child does not feel loved, or when there is little home experience of affection and empathy. It's harder than ever to be a teenager in this affluent world.

Sometimes it is because of external influences that a child becomes at least initially unreachable. Peer group and social media, even one influential friend, can wreak havoc in a teenage psyche. But other times the gap is of a parent's own doing. Too little time and too little attention.

A parent needs urgently to reinvest attention and affection to open up a dialogue of trust gradually. It is worth every effort and not stopping until trust is re-established.

Yet it is altogether another category when parents separate or divorce. The impact can be immeasurably catastrophic. When the love between parents runs out, how can we reassure a young person that love for him or her cannot run out also? Or that even God's love cannot run out?

But when parents do separate, despite perhaps one of the party's best efforts, how can parents at least ensure that a child is not left with a cynical attitude towards love and commitment? Baggage potentially for life.

No couple can take their relationship for granted. What do you do to keep reinvesting in each other? There is so much at stake.

[P for C: 5]

Chapter 3

CLAIMING THE SPACE

'The example of those we love has a mild imperceptible empire and an insensible authority over us; we must either leave or imitate them.'
St Francis de Sales

Talk together

Heart to Heart

Jonathan Doyle constantly challenges parents, 'Claim the space!' You have the right and duty to be the decisive influence in the life of each one of your children but you will need to be work hard if you want this role. Don't surrender the high ground.

Don't be like the dad who put a TV in each of his children's rooms 'just so they can watch a little television before going to bed.' Having strangers in your home is not a good idea. Be decisive. The whole game can hinge on an unthinking decision.

Let us not just spend time with our children but with purpose form their minds and hearts to love wisely and seek truth. Try to go beyond just doing things together, talk, open your heart. Words are necessary. We only know what another person is thinking if they tell us. Build into the relationship with each child a weekly time for trusting one-on-one talk.

Your relationship must reach the point that each of you can raise personal topics. It can be a daddy daughter date, it can be scrumptious afternoon tea with mum, it can be the weekly drive to footy, or McDonald's afterwards; it might be over cocoa on Monday nights, or after a Sunday morning bike ride. Initially it may seem a just a little artificial, but be a good listener, and follow through quickly on promises to help with whatever is needed in the week ahead. What a big challenge this is, but what a blessing when a parent and a child are so close that the young person starts to understand, to intuit, how beautiful must God's love be, because they see a parent's loving affection and understanding up close, every week.

1. What do you do to 'claim the space'?

2. What is your biggest opposition to being the decisive influence in the life of your child?

3. How do you counter it?

[P for C: 16]

Personal and Affectionate Guidance

'Love drives out fear.'
1 John 4:18

'Personal' means reaching the heart. On each row, which of these approaches describes your parenting style? What resolutions can you form and check each week until they become habit? Remember that it can take time to accustom a child to changes. Don't give up... much is at stake.

Impersonal		Personal	
Raised voice at times		Talking quietly face to face so expectations are clear	
Impatient body language		The calmer the better when correcting	
Cold shoulder		Correcting, and allowing a child to start again with no grudges	
Shouting instructions		Asking a child to repeat back instructions	
A home where neither of the adults apologises		Adults and children apologise personally for their mistakes	
Repeatedly asking the same thing		One loving request is sufficient	
Being self-absorbed in the morning or on arriving home.		Always greeting with a smile in the morning and on arriving home	
Do it 'because I said so'		Giving brief clear reasons without argument	
Compel by threatening consequences		Affectionate urgency to impart the skills and character needed for life	
Mirroring a child's emotional state		Bringing your own calm weather	
Sarcasm		Honest explanation of the problem	
Rule based approaches		Fostering personal responsibility	
Arbitrary punishments that have nothing to do with the action		Requiring a child to remedy consequences of a bad behaviour	
Form resolutions that you can check each week over the coming month.			
Resolution Date:			
1.			
2.			

[P for C: 6]

Think About Temperament

Twin studies are important in psychology because they can demonstrate what is genetic and what is learned.

A friend and I had clambered up onto great rolls of hay. He had, one under each arm, his 23 month old identical twins. We were jumping from bale to bale - it sounds more dangerous than it was. 'Here, you take Imi,' he said, passing one of his daughters to me. But Imogen didn't want to be anywhere but in dad's arms. 'OK take Miriam, she is adventurous.' And sure enough Miriam was ready for a new experience, planing along in my arms as if she was on the prow of the Titanic. Even at 23 months they were different personalities. Another mother of 11-month-old identical twins sometimes tells hers apart by their behaviours: one will crawl to the stairs and another at every opportunity will watch the clothes dryer going in circles.

Take this further. The different temperaments of identical twins are not just evident one year after birth, but in the womb itself. One mum says, 'Even in the womb I could tell which twin was which by his behaviour.' Yet how can they behave differently in the womb if they are identical? It seems that epigenetic factors unique to each child, their differential experiences such as early awareness of each other and relative positions in the womb, trigger non-identical genetic development. Individual personality is already being formed from the first months of life in the womb. Amazing.

The behaviour of identical twins can help us to see how important the very earliest input of parents is. Early learning begins in the womb - this accords with a great deal of anecdotal wisdom. One mother jokes of how she used the go to the gym when pregnant, so now the only way to settle the baby is by playing the same bouncy music. Even in the womb, children are affected by their mother's emotions, hormonal responses to people and situations, and diet. Trauma, and distress experienced during pregnancy leave their trace, so why not too, positivity, joy and peace of heart?

Every temperament has qualities that are its strengths and areas it needs to develop, but all temperaments need to learn to love generously without keeping accounts. No child comes into this world with the dedication to others that we need if we are to discover true love.

Here is a simple model of classical temperament with some insights drawn from the work of Alexandre Havard. Bear in mind that most of us are a mix of the temperaments.

The classical temperaments	Features	Natural strengths	Areas to develop
Sanguine	enthusiastic, active, talkative, extroverted	optimistic, social, empathetic,	Fortitude. Strive to be more constant and not overly sensitive, to keep focused on goals and to exercise fortitude

Choleric	independent, ambitious,	decisive, determined, goal-oriented,	Humility. Strive to overcome impulsivity, and impatience, to be centred people than on tasks.
Melancholic	analytical, detail oriented, capable of deep thinking and feeling.	self-reliant, passionate and deeply reflective	Boldness and audacity. Strive to be less self-absorbed, less anxious and more attentive to others.
Phlegmatic	relaxed, peaceful quiet and easygoing.	calm and rational, predictable and constant	Magnanimity. Strive energetically for great goals. Be proactive and generous.

What insights strike you as you read this?

_____
_____
_____

Think about your child's temperamental profile, in particular the areas that do not come easily to someone of their temperament.

What do you see as the natural strengths of your child?	What do you see as the areas corresponding to this temperament that may need to develop?

Cut them slack. Don't judge them. Your child may have to work extra hard in areas that do not come naturally to their temperament.

[P for C: 8]

Now Think About Your Own Temperaments

Share from the heart

Heart to Heart

'Forgiveness is an act of the will and can function regardless of the temperature of the heart.'
Corrie Ten Boom

Think about your natural strengths and the behaviours that come hardest to a person with your temperament. Refer to the table in the previous exercise. It may help to complete a simple online temperament test for example at: https://www.temperamentquiz.com/. Be guided by your spouse. These diagnostic tools only offer an approximate idea.

Mum Temperament:		Dad Temperament:	
What do you see as the natural strengths of your temperament?	What do you see as the areas corresponding to this temperament that may need to develop?	What do you see as the natural strengths of your temperament?	What do you see as the areas corresponding to this temperament that may need to develop?

Reflect on your spouse's temperamental profile, in particular the areas that do not come easily to someone of their temperament. Cut them slack. Don't judge them. They may have to work extra hard in these areas.

[P for C: 8]

Put Yourself in Your Child's Shoes

Share from the heart

Heart to Heart

'Putting heads together to solve a problem or conflict is especially important for avoiding power struggles with strong-willed children.'
Thomas Lickona

How do your children see your relationship? Sit together as a couple, put yourselves in your child's shoes, and agree about what your child sees in your actions. Find evidence for each in the last week.

Characteristic of my parent's relationship	Recent evidence
Mum and Dad laugh a lot together.	
They obviously enjoy each other's company.	
They enjoy doing things together.	
They don't seem to argue, at least when I am around. I never hear them talking loudly to each other.	
They seem to listen to each other with their full attention.	
Every day I see them do things for each other often.	
I see them making plans together.	
Each always seems to know where the other is.	
They are always communicating.	
They have consistent expectations.	
I find their reactions predictable.	
They never ask me to do things they are not prepared to do themselves.	
One never criticises the other when I am there.	
Their faces seem to light up when they see each other.	
They talk really positively of each other.	
Sometimes I see them apologise to each other.	

[P for C: 11]

Things You Both Enjoy Make All the Difference

Learning from others

'Experience teaches us that to love is not to gaze at one another but to gaze together in the same direction.'
Antoine de Sainte-Exupéry

- A friend was concerned that his 14-year-old was dropping off his studies. There were serious red lights: peers were giving poor example; drinking and drugs were part of the scene. He knew his son loved the water so he bought a boat and spent many of the week ends in the next two years with his son, in the boat, having a wonderful time and talking a great deal. The son changed his peer group, picked up his studies. Dad eventually sold the boat. Mission accomplished.
- Another dad rekindled his old love of skateboarding to spend time with his son. After a second broken wrist (along with bruises, sprains and faceplants), he said to his doctor 'I suppose I should give this away!' The wise doctor replied, 'Don't you dare, your son needs you!'.
- An enterprising mum signed up at the local archery club with her hard-to-reach daughter.
- An old rocker invited his sixteen-year-old son to drum for his band; weekly practices, Saturday night club shows, and lots of time together.

What do you enjoy doing with your child?	
Mum	Dad

[P for C: 139]

Correcting with Affection

Prioritise

Heart to Heart

*'It's the old adage: correct in private, praise in public.
Every child is teflon coated when you correct in public!'*
A retired Australian Army colonel, father of seven

Here are some typical parenting traps in correcting children that we need to beware of:

- Sometimes we are sterner than we need to be, even sarcastic; we fail to encourage.
- Sometimes we are not clear enough.
- Sometimes we let too much go and then seem to overreact; we fail to correct things when they are small.
- Sometimes we withdraw affection, failing to adjust our approach depending on the child.
- Sometimes we undermine each other's authority.
- Our corrections are harsh, and we get the same back in kind.
- We want to be fair so we treat every child's behaviour the same; but one has better intentions than the other. We don't seem to take that into account.

Now help each other. Think about times you have corrected your child recently. What do you think your spouse sees in your behaviour when you correct your child?

Mum's reflections. I think this is what my spouse sees when I correct our child.	Dad's reflections. I think this is what my spouse sees when I correct our child.

Compare notes and agree on priorities.

[P for C: 31]

Best Practice Correction

Learning from others

'Pay now or pay later, with interest.'
Jim Stenson

The approaches to correction outlined below have helped many. Consider which you could incorporate? Work through this list with friends.

- 'The calmer the better. Correct calmly. Show self-control, keep the line of communication open and model the behaviour you want your child to adopt. If you do lose your temper, find it before bedtime. Apologise for your part in the fracas. And then listen.'
- 'High expectations integrated with affection will always achieve more than harshness.'
- 'Use No as a loving word.'
- 'Give failures a positive spin. Be positive. Martin Seligman says, "Children need to fail. They need to feel sad, anxious, and angry. When we impulsively protect our children from failure, we deprive them of learning the skills [of persistence]."'
- 'From your emotional reactions draw strength to act, but never allow them to intimidate others. Parents who become angry may obtain compliance with their wishes but in the long run they risk losing the affection, and trust of their child. Children up to teenage years tend the blame themselves if their parents are angry... after that many will tend to blame their parents for lacking self-control.'
- 'Don't find someone to blame. Blame doesn't solve problems. It is a clumsy effort to force someone else to admit guilt, but in the process it blinds us to our own failings and complicates corrections.'
- '"Where there is no love, put love, and you will draw out love," wrote St John of the Cross in the 17th century. Seek to understand. "Put love" means to listen without judging. It means to apologise for the times you didn't listen, or raked up past mistakes.'
- 'Don't correct by nagging. Hear your child out, re-evaluate your conclusions and if you still need to correct, give clear reasons, make the correction calmly and help the child to mend the consequences of his actions—one consequence is worth a thousand words.'
- 'When there is no moral or physical danger, let consequences run their course.'
- 'Without clear evidence to the contrary, always trust a young person's good intentions. Help them see there was another way to get the best result. Your loving trust for a child is the best motivator.'
- 'Keep things in perspective. Don't allow a small matter to escalate. Don't put your son or daughter into a corner with words like: "If you get a bad report then find somewhere else to live." Things said in the heat of a moment can too easily be regretted in the years that follow. Show self-control.'
- 'Pick your battles... be 95% positive with a child.
- 'Remember that your child loves you even when he or she says the most hurtful things. Don't take the harshness personally. Find out what is taking away your child's peace.'
- 'Complement each other. Take over when your partner's approach is not working well.'
- 'Hard lessons can be the best lessons.'
- 'It gets better in the end, if it's still bad, it's not the end.'

[P for C: 22]

Dads and Boys

Set some goals

'Men are not meant for safe havens.'
Robert Kennedy

The goal for dads
- Dad needs to be his son's model of what it means to be a man.
- Boys learn respect for women, and the place of the beautiful gift of sexuality, from dad.
- Dad's (and mum's) example of fortitude is crucial. And in this impulsive age, dad's example of self-control is vital.
- Be aware boys very often follow dad's example of religious practice.
- Dad needs to teach his son how to think: how to manage his impulses, how to react to what happens around him, how to make the right choices and set the right goals, how to truly love God and others.

Why this is not easy
- Dads can be absent from their children's lives because of work or family breakdown.
- The media ensures that the generation gap is alive and well. The peer culture is a world away from parents. Parents' values are not reinforced by the media.
- Fathers and sons have less in common than in the past and spend less time together than in the past.
- Parents can be technologically prehistoric.
- Dads can recycle their own flawed upbringing.

The strategy
- Be closer to your son than any other influence.
- Be objective about the quality of your rapport. Listen to the feedback from your wife. Learn to show affection. Be positive.
- If he does not tell you what is in his mind, you cannot force your way in. Give time and dedication so you have a right to be part of his life. Only then can you talk in depth. Build habits of communication daily and, in more depth, weekly. Identify your behaviours that impede talk.
- Do things together, preferably on things you both enjoy. Build a bank of good memories.
- Have your son in your mind. Know what he is happy and sad about. Know what he is thinking.
- Listen and show affection. Give focussed attention.
- Don't overplay your hand. Form your son to act freely. Correct calmly.
- Work on the humility, dedication, self-control, patience, warmth and encouragement, that hero dads need.

Read, reflect and take one goal away. Share the goal with your wife. Ask her to keep you honest.
The goal I have chosen is...

_____

_____

[P for C: 16]

In the Game

Case study

'No fathers or mothers think their own children ugly.'
Cervantes

> **Strong words for dads who are not in the game:**
>
> *'We talk of leadership – yet we have a whole generation of dads who can't even lead their own family, who can't even lead their own lives. We need a new generation of dads because too many dads don't communicate well, particularly with sons. I mention mothers to my boys and their eyes soften with memories of undeserved favours. You mention dad and there is often a pain born of inadequate relationships. Dads get off the 5.58pm at Epping. They then go home emotionally exhausted. There they hide behind the newspaper or in front of the television. They just haven't got the energy to talk to their sons. This results in another generation of under-fathered boys and it is causing havoc within our society. Too many sons are ending up on a slab with a tag on their toe for want of good mentoring.'*
>
> Dr Tim Hawkes
> For complete article: https://warrane.unsw.edu.au/a-headmasters-view-on-what-we-should-teach/

Let us prepare children so that they too flourish in relationships of love, giving unstintingly as well as taking. Their happiness may depend on these life lessons and example.

1. What would characterize a A^{+++} father-son relationship?

2. What do you have to change to get there?

[P for C: 127]

What Medals does Dad Win?

Take the test

1 GOLD	2 SILVER	3 BRONZE	Which medals does your wife award you? Award the pattern of behaviour not the exact scenario. Use the occasion to set some goals.
Dads who genuinely try to understand their wife's concerns			
			One dad said in a heartfelt way: *'Don't assume you understand what your spouse is thinking. Communicate. This means talking AND understanding. You married because you matched; rediscover this.'*
			The father and mother who always seemed to be thinking the same way, finishing each other's sentences, talking over dinner completely in synch... minds and hearts completely in step.
			The dad who knew how to back his wife calmly when she was emotional.
Dads who are not scared to challenge their kids with affection			
			The dad who said, *'We need to treat every child differently. Each one is very different. Avoid clone recipes for raising children.'*
			The dad whose principle is: *'The more you love them the less you do for them.'*
			The dad whose approach is: *'When you need to talk to an older child about something essential, weather the initial reaction, then they settle down and you can talk.'*
			Another dad whose approach to discipline is: *'The old principle holds: praise in public, admonish in private; children are teflon coated if we correct them in public.'*
			The dad who realizes: *'The more I am grumpy, the more he forgets, the more I praise him, the more he remembers.'*
Dads who care for what comes into the lives of their impressionable children			
			The dad who took out his pliers and cut the cord to the TV (after turning off the power) when his kids broke the family television rule one too many times.
Dads who know how to teach generosity			
			The father who took time off work to paint the roof of the home in summer so he could be extra close to a fragile older child.
			Dad who took his children regularly to see a severely disabled friend who had irreparable injuries from a road accident on pushbike.
			Dad who took his kids to the soup kitchen.
			The father who threw himself into an idealistic cause, giving much time many evenings and weekends, talking about ideals around the dinner table.

Dads who have open communication about the deepest truths of love			
			The dad who says: *'My wife said ask them first what they know. Don't tell them first. They know where babies come from. Ask them what they think the role of dad is.'*
			The father who takes his 13-year-old son on a drive home via a red light district in order to spark deeper conversation.
			The father who takes his son with him for a walk down a seedy area while he carries out a land usage survey at 7am on a Sunday morning. Debrief follows at McDonald's.
Dads who put creativity into family life			
			The dad who bought a season ticket to the Broncos so the family could spend good time together.
			The father who knew how to spark lively, good natured 'arguments' after dinner.
Dads who know how to listen			
			The dad who had a heated exchange with his 16-year-old son who had been thoughtlessly lazy around the home. The dad then accepted the advice of his older daughter: *'Dad, there's an art in deep breathing. Speak softly and you'll win him.'*
			The father who gets the message when his wife says to him: *'You're not looking at him'*. Now he learns to talks or listen to his son giving full attention.
Dads who know how to teach sincerity			
			The father who only ever cranky with his children when they had failed to tell the truth.
			The dad who was embroiled in another relationship and whose mid-secondary son found out about it. He admitted the fault, changed his job to remove the temptation, and talked to his son about what he had done.
Dads who are tough on themselves			
			The dad who exclaims: *'Ultimately how you demand of yourselves will set the limits for your son's development.'*
			The father who didn't lose it when his son was caught shoplifting.
			The dad who said simply to his fellow dads: *'A big issue is that we parents need to learn to say no to ourselves in the way we spend our money... what we do with our money is a lesson for the children, for better or for worse.'*
Dads who are humble			
			The dad, reluctant to buy flowers, whose son told him, *'It's not whether you believe in Valentine's Day but what Mum likes!'* He then changed his mind and bought the flowers.

Here are some dads who did not win medals:

- The dad whose wife realized with concern that her husband's anger on occasions with the baby was an uncanny reflection of her father-in-law's personality.
- The man who says *'Whenever I hear 'A man cannot have two masters!' I think 'two wives.'*

- *'We have been married for 15 years but I cannot talk to my husband. He watches television each night. I need to talk but his attitude is "What is there to talk about?"'*
- The dad who goes to his son's school to complain about unfair treatment when his son did something vindictive to another student.
- The dad who had to be invited by his son to McDonald's for a talk.
- The dad who made excuses for his son who was a fussy eater.
- The father who played too much golf when his children were still school age.
- The dad whose untouched list of jobs to do around the home was a standing joke.
- The father whose most histrionic moments were related to poor school grades.

[P for C: 101]

What a Great Responsibility is Motherhood

Learning from others

'True love begins when nothing is looked for in return.'
Antoine de Saint-Exupéry

Deborah Blum in *Love at Goon Park* documents primate experiments demonstrating the power that mothers have over babies, for better or for worse. Baby monkeys were presented with *mother* dolls, some were cuddly and warm, others cold but with a milk bottle. The baby monkeys repeatedly chose the cuddly *mother* over the cold *mother* even though the cuddly one would not provide milk. Warmth and affection always win.

Yet there was a dark warning in this. She writes: 'The lab team built ... *monster* mothers. There were four of them but they were cloth moms gone crazy. All of them had a soft-centred body for cuddling. But all of them were booby traps. One was a *shaking* mother who rocked so violently that... the teeth and bones of the infant chattered in unison. The second was an air-blast mother. She blew compressed air against the infant with such force that the baby looked ... as if it would be denuded. The third had an embedded steel frame that, on schedule or demand, would fling forward and hurl the infant monkey off the mother's body. The fourth monster mother had brass spikes (blunt-tipped) tucked into her chest; these would suddenly, unexpectedly push against the clinging child. ...No experiment could have better demonstrated the depth and strength of a baby's addiction for her parent. Or how terrifyingly vulnerable that addiction makes a child. These little monkeys would be frightened away by brass spike mom – but then it was she to whom they would still turn for comfort.'

Consider this:

> *Caregivers are in a privileged position of trust. Children will keep coming back even if they are abused, or mistreated, or given terrible example. What great rectitude and determination to give one's best is necessary in a parent.*

[P for C: 57]

Dad Leads the Way

Case study

'Our house rule is that mum shouldn't have to do anything that anyone else can do.'
One savvy spouse

Have some friends over for supper and use this case study as a discussion starter.

> Liriope is talking animatedly to her husband Cephissus as he watches television in the lounge room. 'Narcissus spends so long in the bathroom often there is no hot water for the rest of us. He spends all his pocket money on gel and now even carries a small mirror with him. I don't think this is healthy.' Liri was hoping her husband would acknowledge the problem.
>
> 'I was like that too when I was his age,' Ceph was a little dismissive in his tone.
>
> 'But his grades are going down, there was a *Bigboy* magazine in his drawer, I don't like his friends down the road, and he is starting to use language back to me.'
>
> 'It's all normal for a boy in Year 6, Liri, you worry too much.'
> 'I just wish he would take a good look at himself!' Liri's eyes glistened with frustration at her husband's passivity. 'When was the last time you had good talk with him?'
>
> Ceph reached for the remote control to turn up the volume.

Discussion Questions

1. What are the problems you can see here?

2. Suggest some solutions.

[P for C: 85]

Hero Mums

Learning from others

Read the following quotations.

- 'Honour your mother, and do not abandon her as long as she lives. Do whatever pleases her, and do not grieve her spirit in any way. Remember, son, how she went through many dangers for you while you were still in her womb.'

    Tobias talks to his son. *Tobit* 4:3-4

- 'The wife conceives and carries this burden, bearing the weight of it, risking her life, and giving up a share of her own nourishment; and after all her trouble in carrying it for the full time and bringing it to birth, she feeds and cares for it, although the child has never done her any good and does not know who his benefactor is. ... She goes on rearing him for a long time, putting up with drudgery day and night, without knowing whether she will receive any gratitude.... How much trouble do you think you have given her by your peevish cries and behaviour day and night ever since you were a baby and how often have you worried her by your illnesses? This mother of yours cares for you and does her very best to look after you when you are ill. She makes sure you have all you need, and besides all this, although she is constantly praying to the gods for blessings upon you, you say she is hard to put up with?"

    Socrates to his son Lamprocles in Xenophon's Conversations of Socrates

- Joe, a young dad, was diagnosed with a serious cancer about ten years ago. His mum decided that she needed to do her best to support him in his struggle. She started waking at 3.30am, and praying for over two hours on her knees before going to early Mass. He is now clear of the cancer but she still gets up at the same time to pray. The only thing different now is that she stays on her knees only 20minutes and it is her son who takes her to Mass.

- Annette battled cancer during the 20 years she bore eight children: 'It's not about feeling sorry for ourselves or worrying about cancer, but it's about Him, Jesus, and his redemption. I pray everyday for the cross.' It was this same Annette who decided to walk 100 miles on a pilgrimage while undergoing chemo. She collapsed and had to be taken to hospital. Afterwards she would talk of it saying, 'That was when I was dying in hospital in Canberra that 8th December.' This same Annette, at the graveside of her mother-in-law, at that awkward moment when the formalities were finished, knelt on the ground and started the Rosary. Everyone joined in with her.

Some questions for dad to consider:
1. How do you impress on your children the great heartedness of their mother?

2. Do they witness gratitude in every word you speak to her?

[P for C: 134]

Leadership from Mum

Between sets at Friday evening tennis one player spoke: 'Who does things in life unselfishly? Philanthropists are just like the rest of us. They are in it for themselves.'
'What about mothers... up all night beside a sick infant? Isn't that selfless?'
There was a thoughtful silence

Have some friends over for supper and use this case study as a discussion starter.

> Overheard at a recent morning tea:
>
> 'I only said, "Rasputin, I want to talk to you about your mobile phone bill", and he started screaming and screaming at me as if I was the devil incarnate!"' Alexandra was clearly a little concerned about her son's over-reaction.
>
> 'Yes, my Lear has changed too now that he is in Year 6. He wants everything his own way and won't lift a finger to help after meals. When I threaten to put him out on the street he sulks off to his room for the rest of the night.' Goneril looked very unhappy with her son's lack of emotional control. 'And that husband of mine is absolutely no use. He's never at home at mealtimes to back me up. Mind you I gave him a piece of my mind when he walked in later. The whole street knew how cranky I was.'
>
> Medea chimed in, 'Oh, you've got to be firm. Last night, Jason and I were watching tele and I had to tell my boy that I would rip his bloody arms off it he didn't go back into his room and finish his homework. You should have seen how quickly he moved then!' Medea smiled disarmingly.

Discuss

1. How could Alexandra effectively handle the mobile phone issue?

2. Give Goneril some advice.

3. How could Medea's husband, Jason, make a more effective contribution in his home?

[P for C: 14]

What Would Your Child Say About You?

Share from the heart

Heart to Heart

'This is what a father ought to be about; helping his son to form the habit of doing right on his own initiative, rather than because he's afraid of some serious consequence.'
Terrence, *The Brothers*

What is the dominant impression you are leaving on your child? Here are some real statements from children thinking about their parents:

- 'The patience of my father left a profound impression on me.'
- 'My mother was such a wonderful listener. Every afternoon we would talk.'
- 'My father was a man of few words but he taught me to keep the lectures short. He would say, "Know when you've given enough advice. Mean it and say it".'
- 'I always knew where my father stood on issues. As a teenager I sometimes did not like that. But in hindsight it gave me great security to know my dad's fixed position.'
- 'From my mother I learned the power of kindness.'
- 'The deepest talks I have with my father are about football.'
- 'My mum once wrote to me, '"Remember my son that the only time you are degraded is if you degrade yourself," I have never forgotten that.'
- 'While I was growing up, my dad would often remind me, "Chest out, shoulders back, look the world in the eye."'
- 'My father taught me the meaning of respect. He insisted that we respond with courtesy and did not just shout back through the house if we were being called. Although he came from a poor background, his insistence on education and his insistence on doing our best led us all to university. He insisted that because he was poor we shouldn't smoke, "That's my money, don't just burn it."'
- 'My mother taught me to set high expectations for myself, with the confidence that I can achieve them.'
- 'Mum would always divide portions equally between the children. By doing this she taught us that in a family we're all equal.'
- My father's faith has left a huge impression on me. He came from a country where the faith was persecuted, and the strength of his belief has made all the difference for me.'

Write down what you think your child might say about you, not about your spouse.

_____
_____
_____

Then talk together as a couple and share your self-evaluation with your spouse. Remember: feedback is the food of champions.

[P for C: 161]

Enjoy the Discussion

Parent-child talk

We all have life changing memories of our childhoods. Sharing these memories with your children can bring you closer together and help your child a great deal.

First talk through these questions through with your spouse.

- Who was the person who had the biggest influence on you in your childhood years?
- Talk about the first moments you were transported by beauty, by a movie or an experience.
- Was there a choice could have changed the course of your life depending on your response?
- Think about the hardest lesson you received as a teen or young adult. What made it an effective lesson?
- What was a big mistake you made and how did you recover from it?
- What was the achievement that you most valued as a teenager?
- What setback was hardest for you?
- Who was the person you most respected and why?
- Did you have experience of loss? How did you cope?
- What was the saddest moment for your family during this time? For your father? For your mother?
- What are your best and worst memories of the independence with friends that adolescence brings?
- Who was the best teacher you had and why?
- What did you most enjoy as a teenager? What did you enjoy with your friends?
- What were the character qualities you realised you were lacking as a teen?
- Think about how your parents raised you:
    - What did you see in your parents that impressed you about respect for others?
    - What was the correction, words or punishment, that mum or dad gave you that comes most to mind?
    - What did your father do to teach you to respect others?
    - What did you learn from your mother about saying no to yourself? What memories do you have of your mum's generosity?
    - What did mum and dad teach you about the most important things in life?
- How did you meet your spouse? What were your thoughts when you first met?
- When did you start thinking that perhaps you could spend your lives together?

Now think how sharing these memories one to one with your child. Look for an opportunity, or create it: a daddy daughter date, afternoon tea, a long drive, a special birthday lunch. Find a special time when you are both relaxed and already listening to each other.

The goal is not to talk about yourself *per se*, but to open your heart, and hopefully in return, your son or daughter will open theirs. Remember, humility is gold. Don't big-note yourself in the telling!

Enjoy the conversations.

[P for C: 75]

Chapter 3

Chapter 4

FIX YOUR FACE

'Love gives joy.'
I Peter 1:8

Discuss with friends

Do you come across parents deeply regretful of the example of anger or impatience they are giving to their children? Kids pick up our example and pay it back with interest. They are so adept at reading the *habitual* emotional colour of their parents.

One little girl asked her father who was having a bad day, 'Daddy why are you so angry?'

'What makes you think I'm angry?'

She answered, 'You lifted your eyebrow.'

We have an intuition that our emotional example is at the very heart of the essential life lessons we pass on to children. Let us show abundantly that our family values bring us happiness. Happiness and sadness are key motivators in life; kids learn through our happiness that birthdays, or friends at the front door, and a thousand other things are good things.

Your emotional responses to events and people help your small child calibrate their moral world. Ideally a parent's joy shows that something is good; and from sadness a child intuits that something is authentically wrong. But if your sadness is the result of impatience or moodiness, or your own bruised self-indulgence, how confusing for a child. Your small child trusts you implicitly: impatient example teaches that impatience is justified; moody parents breed moody children. If small children see us angry with them, they will be fearful at first, and unhappy. And when we take that negative emotion from a child into our own responses, we are creating a vicious cycle that breeds further negativity.

Self-management of our emotions not only plays a significant role in teaching children values, but in establishing the culture in our homes. Nobody is more responsible for the parent than the tone in the home, and that tone is established most of all by the *habitual* emotion on the 200cm^2 of your face.

Discuss with friends.

1. Why is effective self-management of our emotional example so difficult?

2. In what situations can positive emotional example become even more difficult?

3. What helps?

[P for C: 26]

Your Own Emotional Example

Take the test

'Show the beauty of the goal, not the toil of the journey.'
Pope Francis

Rate your performance from 0 (woeful) to 10 (consistently marvellous).

____ I put my emotion at the service of others. I use emotion to help others, encourage others, build them up. I avoid self-indulgent negative emotions.

____ My emotional example is both verbal and visual. I choose words carefully. I am mindful of the expression on my face.

____ I teach the difference between a considered response and an emotional response. I help my son or daughter to be mindful of their feelings and emotions.

____ I am passionate about the things I believe in!

____ I avoid correcting when negative emotion is evident.

____ I don't make decisions when I am emotional: 'The more important the decision, the more you do not rush it.'

____ I am mindful of my own 'hotspots'… where fear takes over, or frustration takes over.

____ I sow a positive mindset in the face of life. I show how optimism can and should be realistic.

____ A key factor in relationships is affection. I am not reluctant to show habitual affection to others, loving them as they want to be loved.

____ I am not impulsive.

____ I am very conscious of the emotion coming into my child's life from popular culture, film, and print, and when I don't agree with it, I don't let it get a toehold in my child's outlook.

Total _____

Are you scoring over the 80% mark?

[P for C: 82]

Unsowing Self-Centredness and Self-Indulgence

Case studies

'Love is a mighty power, a great and complete good. Love alone lightens every burden, and makes rough places smooth. It bears every hardship as though it were nothing, and renders all bitterness sweet and acceptable.'
Thomas à Kempis

Invite some friends over to discuss ways in your families to counter these slogans and challenges from popular culture that can mess with your children's heads.

1. 'Just do it!'
2. 'Because you're worth it.'
3. 'Live life to the full.'
4. 'I want my Foxtel'
5. 'All in all it seems the 14 year olds of today are more like the 20 year olds of the '70s…. However one similarity remains, the teenage preoccupation with booze and sex.' Alison Mulvaney-Smith, *Talking with Kids*.
6. 'Feeling good about oneself is so important!' (What else do we need besides self-confidence?)
7. 'He was simply born in the wrong body.'
8. 'Every young person today is inducted as if automatically into two ways of thinking: an ethic of relativism (you have your values but I have mine), and an ethic of autonomy (I'll do what I want)' Prof Hayden Ramsay
9. 'As long as it makes him happy.'
10. 'Vote for love.'
11. 'Be true to yourself.'

Think of other slogans that impact on your child.

_____
_____
_____

[P for C: 86]

Principles of Affective Education

Discuss with friends

Here are some tips for explicit emotional modelling of refined feeling, providing children with the guidebook for what is good and bad in life.

- As human beings our lives are greatly enriched by emotions which enable us to empathise deeply with others and enter into personal relationships, deepen our understanding of situations, and empower us to throw ourselves into great projects.
- If not well managed, emotions can become liabilities. We can be paralysed by fears and anxieties, or become slaves to our appetites for pleasure, power, vanity or possessions. They can distort our view of reality.
- The capacity to manage our emotional lives is at the very heart of character and of effective action. A person enriched by, but not dominated by, emotion is grounded in reality and can set goals accordingly, focussing on others not simply on self-interest.
- Emotion is the grand motivator for most of our actions. We are attracted to what we delight in. We avoid what fear or find difficult. Through the development of the virtues of temperance and fortitude, we learn to manage our emotional lives, and in this way we can choose rather than run on impulse. These virtues enable us to more easily be drawn to what is good for us.
- Our emotional example is at the very heart of the essential life lessons we pass on to children. Happiness and sadness are key motivators in life; kids see our happiness and they learn that birthdays, or jokes around the dinner table, or a thousand other things are good things. They see our sadness at something authentically wrong, and they further calibrate their moral world.
- The whole art form in raising children is to help them find joy in what is good for them. All we say and do leaves a trace. So let us model optimism, and joy in what is good true and beautiful.
- When we give positive and cheerful example, we teach children to stay cheerful and positive. Teach children to make good choices about where they seek happiness. When we model the peace and joy that comes from loving committed relationships, we lay the foundations for the child's future happiness.
- The assumption of a small child is that a parent's behaviour is justified. Older children may see through this and become resentful of parental anger. But either way, the educational result is appalling. If they see us angry with them, they will be fearful at first, and blame themselves.
- Work as a team, giving each other feedback to create culture in the home by the emotional tone of your feedback.

What are one or two conclusions for your family life?

_____

_____

[P for C: 2]

Affective Education in the Home

Our own example is crucial for affective education. Are you implementing their principles? Tick those you wish to focus on.

- ☐ *'If a child has always been given everything he asked for, if his anxious mother always comforted him when he cried, if his child minder always let him do what he wanted, then he will never be able to cope with anything unpleasant in life.'* (Seneca, d. 65AD) Emotional example is all important.
- ☐ *'When I hear an ambulance, my heart goes out to the person inside.'* Our emotional example is delivered first of all by our faces and voices.
- ☐ *'My wife is amazing. The more she is in pain, the more she smiles at me.'* By our faces and body language we know we set the emotional tone in the home.
- ☐ *'My child becomes sad when I show I am stressed.'* We need to be mindful of our initial emotional responses. First impressions leave a lasting impact.
- ☐ *'When the kids are with me I always stop to talk to people asking for help on the street.'* Positive emotions should enrich all our interactions, with family members, friends and strangers.
- ☐ *'When he is upset I run my hands through his hair.'* Affection is always the short cut to build connections and rebuild relationships.
- ☐ *'I hope our kids will adopt our values because they see those values make us so happy.'* We see our own example, and our own emotions, recycled.
- ☐ *'Sometimes I see my spouse in my child's outbursts, and sometimes my spouse sees me in the boy's impatience.'* We need to be mindful of negative emotions clouding our judgement and driving our actions: impatience, anger.
- ☐ *'They hear what we say but they follow what we do'* (Socrates, d. 399 BC) Reason should guide our actions provided it is not justifying hardening of our hearts or walking past someone in need.
- ☐ *'When my four-year-old ran the point of the chisel along the paintwork, I stayed calm.'* In high pressure situations we try to stay courteous and talk with respect.
- ☐ *'My big effort each morning is to greet joyfully each of my children.'* Our good emotional example may not be easy nor perfect but the kids do see us trying.
- ☐ *'We try to fix our faces.'* We are aware of our temperaments. It is sometimes very hard for both us to avoid first reactions but we help each other say sorry in the hearing of the kids.
- ☐ *'We have agreed never to argue in front of the kids as the research flags domestic disharmony as a cause of psychological fragility in children.'* We have a system of agreeing to talk later if our discussion becomes too stressed in front of the kids.
- ☐ *'Strong emotions, such as anxiety, depression, and anger exist for a purpose: they galvanise you into action to change yourself or your world, and by doing so to terminate the negative emotion... When we impulsively protect our children from failure, we deprive them of learning the skills (of persistence)....'* (Seligman) Learning resilience requires encouragement and coaching when there are setbacks.

From the Earliest Years

Prioritise

Heart to Heart

'We always like best whatever we first experience ...and therefore youth should be kept strangers to all that is bad.'
Aristotle

How can mum and dad provide this make-or-break emotional example to infants in the home?

	Dad	**Mum**
Kindness always with a smile.		
Patience even when you are tired		
Calm correction of challenging behaviour		
Example of joyful service		
Example of joyful family interaction		
Showing your delight in order		
Showing the joy of sharing		
Joyful sobriety with respect to food and drink		
Showing the joy in helping		
Affectionate words to child		

[P for C: 124]

Auditing EQ

Prioritise

Heart to Heart

In the table below, you are asked to think about the education of your child's emotions, sometimes this is called EQ, emotional intelligence. Every child is different.

Tick the most appropriate box. What other observations can you add?

All these factors play into education of the emotions. Think about your child's current level of development in each of these categories.	Poor- Better				
This young person is learning to distinguish needs from wants.					
This young person is learning to correct impulsivity.					
This young person is learning to distinguish feelings from convictions.					
This young person is learning to rectify initial reactions.					
This young person has learned to articulate simply and directly if there is a problem.					
This young person has strong habits of respect for others and service to others					
This young person has strong habits of generosity.					
This young person has strong convictions about right and wrong.					
Habits of objectivity in thought are developing in this young person: of critical thinking and not exaggerating problems, of looking at the facts.					
This young person has learned problem solving... breaking a problem into small sized chunks and then addressing them systematically, with realistic optimism.					
This young person has the capacity to set goals for themselves.					
This young person has skills to manage unchecked negative emotion.					
This young person does not escalate their responses to physical actions like hitting.					
This young person enjoys the positive example of siblings, friends, and others.					

[P for C: 83]

Creating a Bright and Cheerful Home

Set some goal

'Forget injuries, never forget kindnesses.'
Confucius

Below you will find family priorities nominated by other parents. Pick two or three ideas in each category on which you would like to keep a focus.

1. What do you think are the main characteristics for an "ideal family atmosphere" that would apply to your home?

    ☐ Having a very united family. Not letting our busy lives stop us from having fun together and creating happy memories.
    ☐ Unity between parents. Unity among parents on strategies for faith and education.
    ☐ Direct involvement by parents in moral education of their children.
    ☐ Creating a culture of kindness, and of respect for privacy, and of each other's belongings.
    ☐ A cheerful home full of good humour. Fun and nonsense. Playing games together.
    ☐ Routines and healthy expectations of contribution and interaction at meal times are essential.
    ☐ Family prayer time. Recourse to God in our joys and sorrows. Daily prayer as a family. Going to Mass together as a family.
    ☐ Sense of tradition. For us it is very important that our children are aware of their heritage and their extended family.
    ☐ Pitching in and co-operation to look after younger ones. Attitude of cheerful co-operation where everyone shares.
    ☐ Let's not be too strict in our families but with the order we need to maintain peace in the home.
    ☐ A home where children learn to speak up, where everybody is encouraged to express their opinion, and everybody listens.
    ☐ A home where we are interested in what each other is doing. The interests and activities of each child are encouraged. We have respect for the individuality of each member and the ability to listen.
    ☐ Discipline is just and in keeping with the misdemeanour.
    ☐ We try to be generous towards each other, sharing, helping with a spirit of service and genuine concern for each other. A home we emphasise focus on each other, not on ourselves, to be courteous and generous with time. On weekends dad strives to create an environment of industriousness.
    ☐ We build an atmosphere where the things everyone does are always done with love. We want our children to see love and affection between us.
    ☐ No TV during the week. Parents read stories and whole novels (in instalments) aloud each evening.

2. What are your strategies to building a positive atmosphere at home?

- ☐ Lots of humour, delegation of work, co-operation, respect for each other, i.e. privacy.
- ☐ Minimal TV (although computers are also a problem). No TV during the week.
- ☐ Help kids to stay busy. We encourage children to participate in extra-curricular activities.
- ☐ Everyone has jobs, set tasks. Older siblings helping with little ones, for example bathing, homework. There is a roster for chores, where all share responsibilities.
- ☐ Children must work for their pocket money.
- ☐ Encourage high academic skills, and help children prioritise their school work.
- ☐ We try to stay focused on our part to improve our children's characters - leading by example (hopefully) and offering lots of affection.
- ☐ Order in daily life. Order and routine. As a family we emphasise that we are a team.
- ☐ We strive to remain calm - no matter what although sometimes we blow it.
- ☐ We ensure there is daily prayer as one family. We occasionally read lives of saints and stories about virtues.
- ☐ Together we review the day over supper.
- ☐ We put a strong emphasis on common activities including cultural and educational activities, for example visiting the science museum, or the art gallery.
- ☐ There is daily time where the older children and parents can communicate without the younger children around us – we have a 9.30 pm supper for parents and teenage children.
- ☐ We emphasise activities where most of the family can have an interest, for example, watching the tennis, on TV.
- ☐ Consistently we encourage children to apologise to each other or to us when something is said or done. We also try to give example in this.
- ☐ We try to have a long-term vision for each of the children.
- ☐ We emphasise to the children how important it is to honour the family name.
- ☐ Our older children know how much we rely on their support. In general we try to respect everyone's abilities and right to contribute.
- ☐ Be available - be there - to allow child to open up, to talk completely trustingly with either of us.
- ☐ Maintain a positive attitude ourselves in our relationship with each other as husband and wife.
- ☐ Husband and wife need to have time for each other on a daily basis and get away for a couple of days every so often – it helps us keep perspective.
- ☐ We avoid yelling out from one room to another. Be in the same room when communicating to ensure you are connecting. And then by establishing eye contact we ensure the child is listening.
- ☐ We have created a tradition over supper of remembering something one is grateful for that day. We need to lead from the front, showing that gratitude brings joy. Then we allow a few moments of personal reflection so we each set a goal for ourselves for the next day. We add a prayer of gratitude, and a moment for personal prayer apologizing for things one could have done better that day and asking for help to fulfil one's resolution.

3. What are the big challenges that need a workaround?

- ☐ Our toughest time was when our first daughter was one and a half. We could not sleep because of interruptions. We were exhausted, grumpy zombies.
- ☐ Weekends can be too hectic for some of the family members, especially with sport.
- ☐ We don't have enough opportunities for sport (adults either).
- ☐ Lack of order.
- ☐ Schoolwork is a battle. We try to encourage greater diligence in schoolwork and order in use of time.
- ☐ Outside stresses can come in and affect the mood of the household. Screens and media tend to invade our family life, especially on weekends. It is a struggle to control the programs.
- ☐ It's amazing the power of consumerism, the impact of brand names and icons of today's

society upon our children, the media push. Even billboard advertising seems to get into our home. We are trying to ensure that our children don't take things for granted in our affluent society.
- ☐ Dad is sometimes very late home in the evening so there is plenty of pressure on time and lack of sleep for mum.
- ☐ Stress from exams and studies can cause tension for individuals.
- ☐ At times the younger children have not yet learned not to be deliberately disruptive. We probably need a reward/punishment system, more consistent and relevant punishments, more one to one talks.
- ☐ Negative influences tend to come from outside the house. We try to be alert for comments that children make which may indicate they have heard or seen an aspect of life that we need to discuss with them, for example a soap which a friend has watched with a story line that presents an anti-family view.
- ☐ Making the most of family meal times is a constant challenge.
- ☐ Our own temperament, even pessimism, seems to affect atmosphere at times.
- ☐ Ideals are not easy to achieve. It is difficult to present family life as positive when older children experience the reality. It can be discouraging.
- ☐ We have lack of space. It is difficult to talk without the children hearing.
- ☐ Some family member are recalcitrant chore dodgers. We need to better monitor our roster system.
- ☐ Intolerance of each other's inadequacies /impatience of children towards each other and of parents towards them can be an issue.
- ☐ Sibling rivalry is a factor in our house.

[P for C: 62]

A Rich Emotional Life

Brainstorm concrete opportunities to teach these predominantly positive emotions to your child.

accepting	driven	modest
admiring	eager	mysterious
adoring	elated	nostalgic
affective	empathetic	optimistic
amazed	enchanted	passionate
amused	enlightened	pleased
anticipating	enthused	pleasant
assertive	euphoric	positive
attentive	excited	proud
attractive	expectant	relaxed
awe inspiring	fascinated	relieved
blissful	focused	satisfied
calm	fond	self-confident
carefree	friendly	self-motivated
caring	grateful	self-respecting
cheeky	happy	serene
cheerful	hopeful	surprised
comfortable	humble	sympathetic
confident	insightful	tender
content	interested	thankful
courageous	jovial	triumphant
curious	joyful	trustworthy
delighted	jubilant	unassuming
determined	kind	vulnerable

Now pool ideas for concrete teaching opportunities arising in relation to negative emotions. Which of the negative emotions that follow can be useful for teaching? Brainstorm concrete teaching opportunities for the appropriate display of the emotions you select.

agitated	embarrassed	lustful
aggressive	fragile	miserly
alienated	fearful	outraged
anguish laden	furious	pessimistic
bitter	gloating	scornful
cynical	gloomy	schadenfroh
dejected	grouchy	sullen
demoralised	hateful	uneasy
depressed	hysterical	vengeful
disgusted	infatuated	vicious

[P for C: 6]

The Extraordinary in the Ordinary

Family activity

Family Meeting

'Let parents bequeath to their children not riches, but the spirit of reverence.'
Plato

Read this testimony of one high-school drama teacher:

'I will never forget one night when I was fourteen. I used to spend Friday nights with my friends, so without enthusiasm one Friday evening I was taken by my parents to see an ancient play called Antigone. I knew nothing about it and had little interest in finding out.

'The thrill of that performance was beyond my imagining. It was a wonderful night. Decades later I can still hear Antigone's voice, the alarm of the chorus, and the moment we discovered her death. I have gone back to that play so many times since. My parents knew better than I.'

Which of these approaches will work in your family and with your kids?

1. Plan a bushwalk as a family.
2. Picnic on a headland on a summer evening.
3. Go fishing.
4. Visit a museum.
5. Attend a live performance or a concert.
6. Go to an art exhibition.
7. Try basic pottery classes and then bring a slab of clay home.
8. Visit a glow worm cave or tunnel.
9. Prepare a visit to a rainforest by researching what to look for.
10. With your children as your travel consultants, plan your next holiday… build anticipation about activities in the area. Research the locations. Pore over the maps. Watch YouTube vision of the places beforehand.

How many extra ideas can you generate with your friends who are also parents?

[P for C: 62]

Sharing Wonder

'Grown-ups like numbers. When you tell them about a new friend, they never ask questions about what really matters. They never ask: "What does his voice sound like?" "What games does he like best?" "Does he collect butterflies?" They ask: "How old is he?" "How many brothers does he have?" "How much does he weigh?" "How much money does his father make?" Only then do they think they know him.

'If you tell grown-ups, "I saw a beautiful red brick house, with geraniums at the windows and doves on the roof," they won't be able to imagine such a house. You have to tell them, "I saw a house worth a hundred thousand dollars." Then they exclaim, "What a pretty house!" That's the way they are. You must not hold it against them. Children should be very understanding of grown-ups.'
Antoine de Saint-Exupery

1. Buy or borrow a microscope. Enjoy the experience together with your child.

Look at all sorts of common objects: salt, sugar, sand from different beaches, hair, onion skin, bread mold, soil, thread, wool, dust, moss, seeds, feathers, grass, pollen, spider webs, fish scales, pond water, and then branch out.

2. Buy a telescope and look at the full moon, Mars, Jupiter and Saturn, and the Milky Way. Binoculars on a tripod can be even better.
3. Take photos in nature. Print and frame your child's best photo.
4. Enjoy a David Attenborough video.
5. Call the kids outside for a beautiful sunset.
6. Create a darkroom (or a digital photofinishing suite).
7. Visit the National Geographic website and look together at the best pictures by year.

How many extra ideas can you generate with your friends who are also parents?

[P for C: 60]

Caring for Nature

Family Meeting

'If a child is to keep alive his inborn sense of wonder, he needs the companionship of at least one adult who can share it, rediscovering with him the joy, excitement, and mystery of the world we live in.'
Rachel Carson

Create an ongoing relationship with nature.

1. Can you teach responsibility by showing your child how to take responsibility for a bird, a cat, or hold the leash each day of the dog?
2. Foster expertise in aquariums and all types of fish.
3. Can you create a veggie garden (YouTube has lots of ideas) and have your child do the watering daily?
4. Bring sunflower seed to maturity.
5. Can you grow beans in a jar on the kitchen windowsill?
6. Or hold a terrarium competition?
7. Or grow potatoes from the eyes on a potato, or carrots from carrot tops?
8. If you are really adventurous create a worm farm.
9. Or build a chook house and feast on the profits.
10. Grow silkworms (find a source of mulberry tree leaves) and watch them turn into moths.
11. Chronicle the action of garden spiders by photographing the web together each day.

Share the interest and derive a double benefit.

[P for C: 132]

Treasuring the Small Conversations About Beauty

Learning from others

It is one afternoon in St Mary's Cathedral, the beautiful neo-gothic sandstone church in central Sydney. The afternoon sun is streaming though the stained glass along the left hand side of the nave. A young mother is carrying an infant, moving from window to window, pointing up at the window, talking gently in the child's ear about the scene. The little child is mesmerized, mum's every word evoking wonder.

Experiences in the first years of a child's life create indelible memories. Children do understand what we are saying even before they can repeat it back. Make the most of these moments. No doubt you have had the experience of saying to a little child even before it can speak a sentence, 'Take this toy and put it in the box.' And the toy is returned to the box.

1. What are the best conversations you have had with your child?

2. How can you take advantage of the small conversations to sow love of family, loyalty, ideals, gratitude?

[P for C: 86]

Via Pulchritudinis

'Every form of catechesis would do well to attend to the 'way of beauty' (via pulchritudinis). ...Every expression of true beauty can thus be acknowledged as a path leading to an encounter with the Lord Jesus.'
Pope Francis, *Evangelii Gaudium*

Pope Francis writes of *'... the inseparable bond between truth, goodness and beauty... a renewed esteem for beauty as a means of touching the human heart and enabling the truth and goodness of the Risen Christ to radiate within it.'*

Let us enrich our children's lives by our enthusiasm for what is noble and beautiful. Let us lead them to marvel at nature and to pause in wonder before art worthy of the name.

Do I show what it means to gaze with wonder at natural beauty? Am I teaching my children to see through the half-truths of manipulative advertising? Of indecent and half-decent fashions? Of political spin? Of peer pressure?

Do I realise that my own joy in what is good, true and beautiful is needed? Children love what we love!

List two initiatives for the coming month in each of the following areas. **The first couple are done as examples.**	
Bringing joy to others	We celebrate Grandma's birthday with handmade cards, poems and songs.
	We weed Auntie Molly's garden next Saturday afternoon and ask her about the flowers she is growing.
Car trips	We picnic on a headland if Sunday is a beautiful day.
	We drive into the city for ice creams on the harbour foreshore one Saturday evening.
Meal times	
Family life	
Family excursion	
Documentaries	

[P for C: 62]

Planting a Love for the Gift of Music

Discuss with friends

*'The man that hath no music in himself,
Nor is not moved with concord of sweet sounds,
Is fit for treasons, stratagems, and spoils.'*
Shakespeare, *The Merchant of Venice*

Beauty should unite not divide. Play a broad range of music in the home from the time the kids are very small. Open your own mind to the whole spectrum of genres, old and new, but call out foul mouthed garbage when you hear it... and explain the reasons, simply. Don't talk out of your hat... do your homework.

When music is a part of your own life it is a gift more easily given. Use music to give joy to others. Yes delightful music, or the mastery of an instrument or piece, gives great satisfaction, but to share in the delight that your music gives others can become a far greater motivator for us.

Plant a love for music. Make music fun for your kids. Through music we pass into a very real world of spirit and beauty. And to plant a love, let us show your own joy.

[P for C: 83]

Divining the Spiritual

Learning from others

Joern Utzon's winning design for the Sydney Opera House defeated 232 other submissions and was proclaimed by the judging panel as a work of 'genius'. Who could doubt this. At his memorial service in 2008, his daughter Lin commenced her eulogy with the prayer that Joern and his wife would recite every day before he commenced his work. She explained that her father believed that all architecture must be inspired by love. Surely this is the great secret of this building. She said that she felt her father's masterpiece was so beautiful that it could almost have been placed there by God himself.

Even a short poem she recited was a testimony to the faith of her father.

> 'Do not stand on my grave and weep.
> I am not there; I do not sleep.
> Do not stand on my grave and cry;
> I am not there; I did not die.'

We cannot but love beauty if we encounter and contemplate it. Beauty and love are inseparable. Both are spiritual values: when shared they are not diminished. And beauty should lead us to the Creator. St Augustine proclaimed, 'only the beautiful is loved'. Think of glorious sunsets and Handel's Messiah. This is the 'way of beauty' that Pope Benedict and Pope Francis have written about.

Wonder is the starting point of every spiritual encounter, an encounter that deeply fulfils our nature with its capacity to inspire love and a certain unworthiness. How can a parent foster this spirit of wonder? Can you teach your child to appreciate natural beauty in different ways every day, from a call of a bird, the dew on a web, a serene moon, the grandeur of a storm, the exuberant colour of a single flower? Do you play music that moves hearts, watch films that uplift, discover a beautiful painting or a tell an encouraging story?

When we go seeking the true, good and beautiful, every discovery is deeply satisfying, be it the beauty of nature or the beauty of a personality. But complacency is a cul de sac that we must not let our lives travel down. When self satisfaction has taken over, there is no room for love.

The way of beauty is a splendid approach to nourishing spiritual depth in a child. Once a noble love becomes part of our psyche, we are drawn repeatedly back. (But sadly the same is true of debased and ugly first experiences.) Goodness, truth and beauty come in so many forms but all will lead to love, and ultimately to divine love. Consider how many of the greatest works of art, architecture, music and literature acknowledge God implicitly and so often explicitly.

Discuss with friends.

1. How can we help children experience genuine goodness and beauty and from this how can we lead them to an intuition of the world of the spirit?

[P for C: 102]

At the Neural Level: Motivation

'Beware of relying too much on artificial rewards. Extrinsic reward undermines the intrinsic appeal of interesting activities.'
Teaching 101

At the core of motivation is the emotional hit we get from carrying out an action. We must therefore raise children to associate positive emotion with actions that are good for them. A parent's job is to expose the child to all that is good, true and beautiful, packaging that exposure in positive emotion. The more genuine the package, the more effective it is - we cannot pass on what we do not possess ourselves.

We do this first of all by managing our own affective example, because a small child is above all emotionally impressionable. So many experiences of an infant are either linked to emotional reinforcement (such as a parent's smile) or to negative emotions (such as parental impatience). Even the youngest of children absorb these emotional events storing them in an area for emotional memories in the brain known as the amygdala. We catalogue things that are desirable or undesirable. When we bring to mind positive emotional memories we trigger dopamine incentives to action. Dopamine is the reward chemical that is the key component in the neural pathways of motivation. But this incentivisation can be associated with good actions (such as helping others) or damaging actions (such as eating too much, getting even, unleashing our anger etc); parents and educators have a duty to ensure that children only develop reward expectations that are actually good for them.

Mirror neurons, the automatic mechanisms for imitation of actions and emotions, also play a part here. Through them we intuit the emotions of others by living out those emotions in our own skins. Hence, emotion is contagious. Our emotions affect others for better or worse. We must manage our responses to what happens around us.

The task of an educator is to teach refined attitudes to pleasure and difficulties, to teach children to seek pleasures to the extent they are truly good for us and put up with difficulties when there is a sufficiently good reason to do so. First we adults must manage our faces; pay attention to others, reflect the joy of a character that is at peace with itself. Encourage, and correct calmly... the calmer the better. Our example is crucial. All of us involved with young people have a duty to stay joyful.

1. Consider specific behaviours that you are encouraging in your child. How can you ensure that these behaviours have a positive emotional association in your child's mind?

2. On occasions we can help a child become more conscious of positive emotion by pointing it out. For example, 'How did you feel when you helped your little brother?' Think of a range of contexts where this approach could be effective.

Chapter 4

Chapter 5

THE BUILDING BLOCKS OF CHARACTER

Discuss with friends

'The more you love your children, the less you do for them'.
John McMahon

Fr Chris Riley has been legendary because of his tireless assistance and advocacy for homeless youth.

When Fr Chris arrived at my school to talk to parents and students, he arrived in his mobile office, complete with hound. We offered him lunch, which he refused, but were able to put a cup of tea in front of him. But as soon as he sat down, a boy came to announce that the assembly of parents and senior students was ready. I said, 'Take your time, Father Chris, finish your tea.' But jumping up he announced, 'Life's too busy to spend it drinking tea,' and we went to the hall.

He talked about the plight of homeless kids, about young people hooked on drugs before they can think clearly, of girls rescued from the street. There were many moving stories. He understood that we need to be moved by hearing about the suffering of others. Compassion is an emotion. Then he urged parents, 'Have the courage to demand greatness from the children in your care.' Character building starts at home, and it requires the courage of day-in and day-out dedicated parenting.

Virtues are the building blocks of such character. The goal is self-mastery, to run one's own life, so that one can truly love others and possess peace of heart. The family, where an overriding motivation is the welfare of the other members, is the environment *par excellence* for fostering virtue. In a family, love for others is the most natural motivation for service.

Early childhood

In a young child the foundations of virtue are built by example, encouragement and affection, by clear consistent guidelines, routines, close follow up, and by punishments based on consequences and imposed without anger.

Our goal is to build habits. Plutarch understood this: 'Character is established habit,' he wrote. And in the Christian heritage the same rules apply; St Thomas Aquinas insisted 'Habits are necessary in order to act well.' Routines and order are the building blocks of habit, and habits motivated by love are virtues: 'Rufus, mum would be so grateful if you could help her when you get home this afternoon. She has a very busy evening.'

Teach love first of all by your affective example. Children learn their emotions first of all from mum and dad. Their emotional example in face, tone of voice and body language teaches us what to love and what to avoid in life.

Build habits of obedience? Why is obedience so important? Aristotle puts it so simply: if children have learned to obey the reason of their parents, they will be able to obey their own reason as they grow.

> *'The evil begins at home; for when they are boys by reason of the luxury in which they are brought up they never learn, even at school the habit of obedience.'*

This insight goes to the very heart of character building: the natural impulsiveness and fearfulness of a little child is conditioned so that it learns to stop when asked, put up with the discomfort of getting up and helping, etc. There are parallels here with the way that we train a puppy to obey by conditioning its responses. It learns to act in accord with its master's wishes... to sit, to fetch, to beg, to stop barking, to attack, etc. When a child is trained, not only is childish impulsivity redirected to follow a parent's directions, but progressively a child is enabled to give himself or herself good reasons for action.

Children are given a marvellous head start by their parents when they have learned obedience very early in their lives. A friend of mine takes his two year old Anton in his arms and says simply, 'Anton sleep!' Anton immediately puts his head down and shuts his eyes. It may be a party trick, but there is no doubting Anton's obedience. Stay calm, constant, and insistent. The child who learns to obey will later manage their own impulses with their own choices.

Later childhood

When a child is older the focus continues on building orderly routines. Clear parental expectations are important, but educating a child to act from loving motives becomes more important. Children can be helped to reflect on their own actions by asking them to make certain decisions by themselves. We can help them develop a positive mindset by showing them how to learn from mistakes, taking them in their stride and having an optimistic view of difficulties. When they are still necessary, punishments should help remedy the consequences of ill-chosen actions: 'Odette, it's really important to learn how to wash dishes thoroughly so the meat is not still stuck to the plate. Let's do them again.' Or, 'Brutus, what a pity that you didn't listen when I asked you not to play cricket near the windows. Will I take the money from your account, or do you want a cut in your pocket money until it is paid off?'

In these years children are able to take far more responsibility for their own character improvement. They respond very well if encouraged to act from motives of charity towards a parent or one of their sisters or brothers. Home atmosphere and family example continue to play a major role, consolidating the habits acquired in earlier years. The value of a positive peer group becomes very noticeable also at this time.

Teenage Years

In teenage years, a boy or girl develops the adult capacity for independent action based on personal conviction. It is good and natural that teenagers should want more and more freedom and autonomy; it is a prerequisite for a mature personality. Parents should not be scared when they observe a growing independent spirit in their son or daughter. They should not react with panic and legislate rules as if their teenager were still a child. Nor should they retard the development of their offspring by smothering them with childish pampering. Nor should they look on fondly as their teenager exhibits every sort of silly, superficial behaviour, naïvely justifying it with words such as 'kids will be kids'. Confront this issue: 'Oh Stevie, those IronCarnage posters will give your little sister nightmares. I'll get you to take them down'. Encourage teenagers to act out of love for others.

Virtues are not fostered impersonally. A teenager will grow in virtue because he or she is encouraged personally, to improve, to seek higher ideals, and to act from better motives. Parents must be close to each child, talking frequently and confidently to their teenage son and daughter so that they can provide this affectionate encouragement. Only if such a close relationship exists will the firm, clear guidelines needed in teenage years be trustingly accepted. And only through such a close relationship will the parent have sufficient sensitivity and understanding for their teenager's thoughts and feelings, and sufficient respect for his or her legitimate freedom.

The foundations for such a relationship are sown in the friendship and time spent together in childhood years. Have character goals for each child. Talk about them as a couple. Pray about them. Review them every week and lead by example. In summary we read in the *Catechism of the Catholic Church*. 'The moral virtues grow through education, deliberate acts, and perseverance in struggle. Divine grace purifies and elevates them.' (1839). The development of virtue takes time, like every other worthwhile victory. So stay in the game.

1. What do you see as the character-building priorities for parents of infants?

2. When their children are in the stable years of childhood, what can parents talk about in their regular conversations together to plan their parenting points of focus?

3. How can parents of teens build close trusting relationships with their sons and daughters? What factors seem absolutely decisive?

[P for C: 40]

All Our Behaviours are Self-Reinforcing

Reflect

'Young men have strong passions and tend to gratify them indiscriminately.'
Aristotle

We have all noticed that the more we get up at a certain time the easier it is to do so. The routines we establish in the morning facilitate us getting out the door on time. Repeated behaviours consolidate neural pathways for those behaviours. The more we do something the easier it is to do it, or to fall back into doing it. This can be good or bad.

We can use this understanding to great advantage to change our own behaviours, by substituting better behaviours, and also to form behaviours in a young person who is in our care.

The first step to changing our own behaviour is to be specific about the issues. It can help to think in terms of positive (oriented towards others) emotions, or self-indulgent emotions.

- Are there occasional emotions that I want to eradicate from my personality?
- When do my thoughts prevent me giving my best to others?
- Are there times in my schedule am I more likely to be preoccupied, paying poor attention to members of my family?
- What are the emotions that I want to show to my family every morning?
- Are there times in my day when I do not give my full attention to my loved ones who are at my side?
- When do I complain?
- When do I lose patience?
- What are the times and places where my attention becomes caught on things that are not helpful (negative news scrolling, fixations about the behaviour of others, online shopping catalogues, Facebook and Instagram browsing, etc)?
- When I am not as cheerful as I can be? When do I allow self-pity in?
- When am I resentful? When do I become indignant or defensive? Can I substitute habits of direct but courteous response?
- When should I speak up more for the good of others?
- Do I have habits of speaking about others without respect?
- Do I allow insincerity into my life? Have I allowed myself to think one thing but say another? Do I manage my impulses and temperament, avoiding impulsive anger?
- Am I convinced that I should tap into my feelings but they are not good guides? Do I maintain dominion over my feelings and emotions?

Now consider how you make use of this in parenting:

- What positive behaviours in your child are you seeking to encourage?

_____

- What negative patterns of wanting and desiring are you noticing?

  _____

- What negative patterns of talking are you noticing?

  _____

- What routines do I establish for my child as a scaffold for good habits?

  _____

- What negative habit-forming behaviours and activities am I noticing: excess collecting material things, excessive TV viewing and computer games, curiosity on the internet, snacking at will, habits of talking negatively of others, habits of ducking out of jobs, habits of 'forgetting', habits of letting someone else do it or take over, habits of quitting, of laziness, habits of not telling the truth, habits of wanting to be the centre of attention?

  _____

[P for C: 65]

Character is on the Inside

Reflect

'...nothing but the courage and unselfishness of individuals is ever going to make any system work properly. It is easy enough to remove the particular kinds of graft or bullying that go on under the present system: but as long as men are twisters or bullies they will find some new way of carrying on the old game under the new system. You cannot make men good by law: and without good men you cannot have a good society. That is why we must go on to think... of morality inside the individual.'
C. S. Lewis

Laws can't make us good nor can bad company take away personal responsibility, even though poor parenting has a lot to answer for. Are you winning the battle for the heart and mind of your child?

In what ways is this quote relevant to family life?

_____
_____
_____

[P for C: 42]

What are Virtues?

> 'Human virtues are firm attitudes, stable dispositions, habitual perfections of intellect and will that govern our actions, order our passions, and guide our conduct according to reason and faith. They make possible ease, self-mastery, and joy in leading a morally good life. The virtuous man is he who freely practices the good. The moral virtues are acquired by human effort. They are the fruit and seed of morally good acts; they dispose all the powers of the human being for communion with divine love.'
> **Catechism of the Catholic Church**

Only one of the statements below is not true. Which one?

____ A virtue is 'a habit of choosing well'.

____ Virtue 'is what makes its possessor good and his work good likewise'.

____ Virtues are 'perfections of the human character'.

____ Virtues are acquired by repeated acts carried out with the right intention.

____ A virtue is a disposition in one's character to act consistently in a particular way for a good motive.

____ Virtues enable self-management.

____ Virtue enables us to think clearly and judge wisely.

____ Virtue empowers us to say 'no' to pleasures and distractions that are not good for us.

____ Virtue empowers us to say 'yes' to challenges that are worthwhile.

____ Virtue leads us away from self-indulgent, self-centred, and self-serving actions and towards a way of living that is attentive to others.

____ Virtues make us free because they help us to be self-directing, free of negative impulses external influence.

____ Virtue is decisive in achieving human fulfilment.

____ Virtue is decisive in achieving peace of heart.

____ A virtue is a good habit.

____ Virtues have nothing to do with good habits and strengths of character.

[P for C: 44]

Virtues are Good Habits

Prioritise

Heart to Heart

Remember: habits are developed by repetition. Assess the quality of this consolidation.

A CHECKLIST FOR CONSOLIDATING GOOD HABITS	Level of Development in your family					Priority areas
	Well developed	Fair to middling	Fair	Much work needed	Non-existing	
We emphasise routines and consistency in the home.						
We delegate even if it takes more time to get the job done.						
We insist that our child acts with a loving intention.						
We address bad behaviours before they become habits.						
We find ways to help our child think for himself or herself ... asking preferences, opinions and goals.						
We each strive to give the best example we can, all the time.						
We clearly teach what is right and wrong.						
We focus on building up habits in our child's younger years.						
We make character building the aim of our child's sport.						
We turn parenting crises into opportunities to build character.						
We greatly value sincerity in our home.						
We correct small and large insincerity.						
We are conscious of our own example in matters relating to sincerity and honesty.						
We value greatly generosity in our family.						
We teach a deep respect for others.						
We have created a culture of generosity in the home.						
We teach detachment from material things.						
We strive for practical solidarity with those who are less fortunate.						

[P for C: 46]

Consider the Motivation

'Through virtues we deliver love to others.'
Dr Donald DeMarco

Good character doesn't put on a show, it is true service even when it seems that no one else is involved such as when we are studying with intensity. For example, preparing ourselves to be a good professional is an act of service. We can't be in it for ourselves. We can't put success, or popularity, or praise, above helping others.

In other words, for virtuous acts it is important not only that the action be good but the motivation must be good also, and the person must act freely - without coercion or without any other effective choice. The bar is quite high. Part of the task of parenting is to help young people cement a habit of right intention into their behaviours.

So, a young person who tells the truth must learn to do so out of love for the truth itself, and love for the other person, not just to get out of trouble.

1. Think about your example. And think about how you encourage care of others. Think about the intention you see in your child's obedience, helpfulness, sincerity, or determination.

2. Are there any indicators that sometimes your child can still purify the intention with which they act?

3. Think about this and then discuss what you are seeing over a long cup of coffee.

[P for C: 74]

Virtues are Actions with a Loving Intention

Family activity — Family Meeting

Nominate a month to highlight virtues. Don't make it a competition but create cards with the names of virtues to highlight virtues such as:

Prudence	Justice	Fortitude	Temperance
Seeks truth and reality	Respectful of all	Courageous	Self-control
Discerns good from bad	Responsible	Magnanimous	Detachment from things
Able to set goals	Compassionate	Patient	Cheerful
Sincere	Generous	Persevering	Sober
Flexible with respect to opinions	Attentive to others	Resilient	Pure of heart
Seeks advice	Obedient	Industrious	Modest
Reflective	Grateful	Orderly	Enthusiastic
Idealistic	Able to forgive without grudges	Persistent	Serene.
Mindful of own feelings	Leads others	Calm	Mild
Humble	Empathetic	Determined	Moderate
Optimistic and hopeful	Diligent	Ambitious to do good	Able to temper curiosity
Confident	Courteous	Forthright	Capable of awe and wonder
Decisive	Spirit of service to others	Honourable	Detached from opinions
Wise	Kind to all	Daring	Possessing peace of heart

When you have spotted the child performing a virtuous action, recognize it, make the card:

- ☐ 'I showed FORTITUDE when I ... (put my toys away when I was tired, etc)'
- ☐ 'I was ATTENTIVE TO OTHERS when I...'
- ☐ 'I was PRUDENT when I ...'
- ☐ 'I showed SELF-CONTROL when I ...'

Then post it up and celebrate with a small reward.

In the process teach the child that a loving intention in the action is really important.

[P for C: 48]

Teach a Loving Intention Explicitly

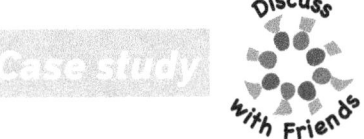

Case study

'One month with afternoon cartoons and we saw an identical change of character in each of our three kids. It took them two weeks to come back to normal after we got rid of the cartoon channel and its silly violence.'
One parent's comment

Look at the table below. Tom is helping his mother with the washing up. Robert and Nicole are doing homework. All are working to the best of their abilities, but only Tom and Nicole seem to be working with a loving intention. They are working to please their parents, and in addition Nicole sees her school work as building the skills to serve others in the years to come.

The table separates action, the underlying virtue, the quality of the action itself, and the intention in carrying out the action.

	Action	Virtue	Quality of the action itself	Intention in the child's mind
Tom	Doing the washing up	Generosity	Working carefully and attentively	Desire to help mum.
Robert	Doing homework	-	Working carefully and attentively	Avoid getting into trouble at school
Nicole	Doing homework	Diligence	Working carefully and attentively	To please parent and to better serve others in the future.

1. What could you say to Robert to help him work for a nobler reason?
2. Think of your own child. In what actions do you see that a loving intention may be lacking? How can you encourage your child to put a loving intention into helping or into school work?
3. Think of your own example. Does your child always see good example in your work about the house and in your professional work?
4. What could you say to your child to help them realise how to rectify their intention and act for less self-centred motives? If you are a family of religious faith, consider how the simple practice of a morning offering helps us to act out of love of God and others.

[P for C: 74]

Audit the Simple Courtesies

Take the test

When we don't work at simple courtesies we end up taking others for granted.

1. Virtue requires intentional attitude of care for others. Think of these questions about your own example:

   ☐ How often do you explicitly say please?
   ☐ Do you always thank others for the smallest help?
   ☐ Do you readily apologise?
   ☐ Do you keep your commitments?
   ☐ Are you aware when your spouse or one family member has a particularly tough day?
   ☐ Do you step in to help without being asked?
   ☐ Are you habitually courteous?
   ☐ Do you refine a generous home culture of smiling service to each other, of offering to help?
   ☐ Do you readily take over when someone is tired?
   ☐ Are you conscious of not leaving mess for others to clean up?
   ☐ Do you ring if you are going to be late?
   ☐ Are you punctual out of a desire not to waste others' time?
   ☐ Do you get home on time and so communicate your great desire to be with your family?
   ☐ Do we each dress well as a mark of respect for others?
   ☐ Do we clean ourselves before dinner as a mark of respect for others?

   Score yourselves on one day. Ask your spouse to help. Keep it simple. Take note when you say 'please', 'thanks' or 'I'm sorry', to anyone in the house. Compare notes at the end of the day. Then help each other to improve in the domains you realise you need to work on.

2. Your child needs the courteous habit of paying full attention to whomever is talking to them, of greeting while looking in the eye, of not walking past someone without a smile and a greeting, of allowing another to pass through a door first, of excusing themselves if they need to interrupt, of not shouting indoors, and of using polite modes of address with courtesy and poise.

Teach these skills repeatedly until they are second nature.

   ☐ Establish expectations of greeting mum on arriving home, of ringing if one is going to be late, of not keeping others waiting, of dinner together, etc.
   ☐ Enlist the help of grandpa to teach a child to shake hands and look a person in the eye.
   ☐ Have children look after visitors to your home, teaching them all the courtesies of bringing visitors in, offering refreshments, not leaving them unattended, etc.
   ☐ Teach children to make phone calls courteously and to make polite purchases on your behalf.

[P for C: 15]

Do I Live and Breathe a Loving Mindfulness?

Take the test

'If your emotional abilities aren't in hand, if you don't have self-awareness, if you are not able to manage your distressing emotions, if you can't have empathy and have effective relationships, then no matter how smart you are, you are not going to get very far.'
Daniel Goleman

Can you tick these 10 boxes?

- ☐ Do I have a healthy intentionality about my actions? Do I know what I want? Or am I driven by a jumble of unprocessed and unprioritised impulses and desires?
- ☐ Do I know how to live the moment... immersing myself in loving conversation with my family, delight at a beautiful evening, gratitude on waking up to so many blessings?
- ☐ Do I exercise self-regulation? Do I model mastery of temperament and impulse: especially considering that poor emotional control is self-reinforcing?
- ☐ Do intentional choices guide my day and my life's course? Do I understand and teach that our choices make us who we are?
- ☐ Do I master my scattered attention and fragmented day?
- ☐ Do I understand that self-mastery opens the door to self-giving? Do I try wholeheartedly to give my attention to others and their needs?
- ☐ Do I put my head and my heart at the service of others by understanding the role of good habits and virtues?
- ☐ Do I teach positive self-talk to put positive emotions at the service of those around me?
- ☐ Do I teach skills to derail unwanted direct emotional reactions: change point of attention, switch on the cognitive pathways by focusing on facts? "Don't rush in. Think about it!" Buy time. Use paper. Ask advice from others. Pray about big decisions.
- ☐ Do I identify patterns of impulsiveness without giving myself excuses?

[P for C: 25]

Make the Virtue Concrete

Family activity

Family Meeting

'(Virtues are) strengths of character that make the good life possible.'
Martin Seligman

1. Over dessert on one night of the week have everyone tell a story of a virtuous action they have witnessed during the week.

   Vote on what was the most heroic action and reward the person who spotted it with an extra dollop of ice cream, or by doing the job they like after dinner.

   Do this with your friends to build up a library of inspiring stories you can retell at home.

2. Come prepared to talk about an inspiring figure from real life, or to read an inspiring passage from a novel poem (think of the great ballads) or play.

   Invite your children to do the same.

   Recount your story or read your passage, then with your children, brainstorm the virtues that are illustrated.

   For each, can you think of other similar stories which illustrate the particular virtue in action?

   Have the family discussion about ways that we all can live the virtue that has been identified.

   [P for C: 48]

Mistakes are Opportunities

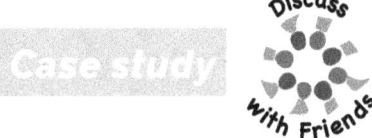

Case study

Perhaps we should not be so quick to throw our hands in the air when something goes wrong. When Rafael Pich, parent educator, father of 16, and everyone's kindly grandfather, came to Australia to run seminars for parents he insisted that when a problem manifests that is a good thing. It was a problem that was waiting to happen, but below the radar... but now that it is in the open it can be dealt with. Failures are opportunities.

Here is a real-life case study that demonstrates this:

> A mother and daughter were in transit for a few hours to change international flights. The 13-year-old daughter, browsing in duty free, took a fancy to some expensive accessories and slipped them in her bag. The shopkeeper who had seen her, asked once, 'Is there anything you wish to buy?' She said 'No', walked out, and was immediately arrested by security. She was charged and spent the night in custody. She and her mother missed their flight.
>
> This led to long deep conversations with her mother, and since then she has not looked back. It was a total turning point. Prior to this incident she was a somewhat distracted and lazy student, and much more interested in social life after school. This event was just the wakeup call she needed. She finished school as an exemplary student and now is a highly successful young professional very much involved in helping others.
>
> Full marks to her mother, who no doubt was bitterly disappointed but who reacted calmly and supported her from the start to form a practical game plan, providing all the personal support required. Together they turned this apparent disaster into a massive win.

1. Suggest three typical everyday catastrophes in raising children?

2. Visualise how these can be turned into opportunities.

3. What can stop parents from turning such setbacks into wins?

[P for C: 91]

Being Specific About How to Change

Prioritise

Heart to Heart

Think in terms of guided practice that you lead a child through, goals they set for themselves, and behaviours you wish to correct.

The specific virtue we wish to encourage in our child:_____	Strategies
Opportunities for guided practice:	1. 2. 3. 4.
Goals we will help our child set for himself or herself:	1. 2. 3. 4.
Behaviours we will correct kindly but resolutely:	1. 2. 3. 4.

[P for C: 131]

Are You Raising a Leader?

Beneath the best leaders we find confidence, clear-headed self-possession, a deep sense of responsibility and duty, a personal humility and a profound respect for others. Such qualities are the total opposite of the lightweight superficiality and the absence of care that characterises the worst of politics and hype marketing. Real leaders project themselves authentically... the face they show others reveals the person they genuinely are.

- Are you encouraging the strengths of character in your child that leadership demands: wisdom, sincerity, courage, generosity and spirit of service, responsibility, humility, calmness, cheerfulness, the capacity to fix one's attention on a goal, and practical optimism?
- Do you talk about inspiring examples?
- Are you teaching the knowledge that leadership demands? For example do you talk about the qualities of great leaders and how they overcame difficulties? Do you teach critical thinking?
- Do you foster a depth of empathy for others? Are you raising a young person of reflection?
- Are you developing the skills in your child that leadership demands: the ability to articulate convictions, the courage to talk in public, and the capacity to motivate others?
- How do you inculcate in your child energy and the capacity to get things done, to effectively prioritise.
- Are you conscious that a young person's present habits of courtesy and concern for those around them will determine, to a very large extent, the quality of the positive contribution they will make to fellow man in the years ahead.
- Are you mindful that this generation of young people will be in a position to leave their mark on society, for better or worse, in only ten or fifteen years' time, for some even less. The clock is ticking.
- Are you doing all you can to ensure that habits of selfishness, of over demandingness, and of off-handedness to others do not take root in the young persons in your care?
- Are you striving to lead by example... to demonstrate by your actions that leaders do not ask their followers to do anything they are not prepared to do themselves?

Now summarise your game plan in these two tables:

Evident leadership qualities	Qualities for development
Where we show this example	**Where we can improve**

[P for C: 140]

At the Neural Level: What is virtue?

Learning from others

Small children require 'critical experience', guided and appropriate training, taking place at the right time.'
Nancy Sherman, *The Fabric of Character*

Virtues are established good habits. Neurobiologically in the simplest terms, they consist of consolidated neural pathways of behaviour, consistent with training of our reward and aversion systems. For example consider, how by conviction and repeated practice, we can train ourselves to a positive first reaction when you notice that someone needs help, for example, that your child wants your attention.

A virtuous person is a person both master of and enriched by emotions. Emotional regulation is at the heart of virtue because all too easily our emotional state can derail good decision making: paralysed by fear or driven by reward conditioning attuned to the wrong stimuli, we are not truly free and master of our own soul.

The state of virtue is characterised by a grand integration of systems in the brain that mediate rich emotional experience with cognitively based decisions. It is the best of both worlds. The neural signature of virtue incorporates the systems and pathways for regulation of both fear and reward seeking emotional responses, of cognitive goal election, of consideration of consequences, of imitation and empathy, of attention (which is so linked to the will power) and of habit formation itself.

This integration is possible because of the capacity of the brain to modify according to experience and environment. This takes place through a constellation of processes associated with experience-induced neural plasticity. The development of virtue is essentially a learning process whereby the brain is structurally modified to reflect consolidated and dominant neural pathways. Systems mediating attention, imitation, early learning and neural development, emotion processing, fear response, reward and goal election, and habit formation all play their coordinated parts. The subcortical basal ganglia as well as areas of the prefrontal cortex appear to be important brain regions related to the formation of intentional habits, and cognitive processing of emotion.

All thoughts, desires and actual behaviours predispose us to further thoughts, behaviours and actual desires of the same type. The more one thinks, desires or acts in specific ways, the more these thoughts, desires and actions are hardwired into our personalities. This has grand implications for the education of small children.

1. For better or for worse, the more we carry out a certain behaviour, recall a certain emotional memory, entertain a specific desire, or channel our attention in a particular direction, the more that action is reinforced. Past behaviours become the best predictors of future behaviours. Nominate specific scenarios where you want to consolidate particular behaviours, memories, desires, or habits of attention.

2. Once a negative behavioural pathway is established and we wish to overcome that behaviour, it is a matter of consolidating a more positive behaviour as a preferred pathway. This takes time. Think of negative behaviours in this category.

Chapter 6

CARDINAL VIRTUES

'Grace builds on nature, it is impossible to grow in grace if you don't live the cardinal virtues of prudence, justice, temperance and courage.'
Steve Markel, founder of Families of Character

Discuss with friends

Character is built on four pillars: self-control, fortitude, respect and responsibility, and sound judgement. The pre-eminent role of these four habits has been the accepted wisdom not only in the western world for two and a half thousand years, but in almost every other culture. This understanding accords with the work of Martin Seligman (and the approaches of Positive Psychology), with clinical psychological practice, and also with neuroscientific studies that have identified the brain systems underpinning our reward conditionings and capacity for goal election, processing of fear responses, and conscious habit formation, along with our cognitive management of emotion, attention, imitation and empathy.

With these four master-virtues, one is fully equipped. They are known as the cardinal virtues, the four habitual dispositions that best prepare human beings to cope in whatever situation they are in.

- Prudence, sound judgement, plays a guiding role. Aquinas understood prudence as the perfection of conscience, the habitual readiness to make decisions based on reality, the recognition that the goal of our lives is to love what is good and accomplish it. It is the source of sincerity and humility.

- Justice, also sometimes called respect and responsibility, is the very habit of choosing well. Our every action is carried out taking into account our duties to others, first of all to God but also to family members, friends and all mankind. Justice is the source of generosity, piety and religious and filial duty, and ultimately happiness. 'The door to happiness opens outward,' Kierkegaard concluded. We must focus on others if we wish to be happy.

- Fortitude and Temperance are our trained emotional responses, without which our reason is easily hijacked. They are the well-described conditionings in our reward expectations and in our responses in fearful and difficult situations so that these emotional responses to pleasure and pain readily accept the guidance of reason.

Without the emotional management of temperance and fortitude there is no possibility of rational choices, and if justice is lacking, our otherwise rational choices will be self-serving. Virtue is an all or nothing affair. The more we interiorly struggle to be virtuous, the more easily we connect with others, the better our choices in relationships, the better our choices in life, the more able we are to seek God, and the happier we are.

[P for C: 50]

Which Cardinal Virtue is Which?

For well over two thousand years, since the time of Socrates, human beings have striven to develop themselves in the four great domains of character that are known as the cardinal virtues. Two empower us to manage our emotional lives (our appetite for pleasure and aversion to pain and difficulty), and two help us think clearly, and choose wisely, infusing every choice with love of others. All the other virtues can be grouped within these four cardinal virtues.

Every human being needs these habits. Without the cardinal virtues we cannot think, judge or act rightly. Without a conviction in the importance of truth, without deep desires to orient my life to others, without appetites which are well trained, I will end up misguided, selfish, and pulled in every direction by my feelings.

Place the four virtues above their correct description below.

The habit of seeking, paying attention to and delighting in, all that is good, true and beautiful, so that we direct ourselves only to what is good for us, saying 'no' to, or moderating, our desires for things that are not good for us.	The habit of managing our fears and confronting difficulties in the face of worthwhile but challenging goals. In its complete development it means to apply ourselves with perseverance and peace of heart in striving for great goods that are very difficult to attain.	The habit of choosing so that we give others what they have a right to and maintain a diligent care and respect for all. In its full development, it is the habit of infusing every single choice and action with love of others.	The habit of seeking the truth, living in reality, informing ourselves of what is right, of setting goals appropriately, living in reality, and of informing ourselves about what is right. It is the virtue that guides all the other virtues.

Brainstorm persons who exemplify each of these virtues.

Temperance	Fortitude	Justice	Prudence
1.	1.	1.	1.
2.	2.	2.	2.

[P for C: 50]

An Initial Audit of the Cardinal Virtues

Prioritise
Heart to Heart

REVIEW YOUR CHILD'S GOOD HABITS	Level of Development in your family					Priority areas
	Well developed	Fair to middling	Fair	Much work needed	Non-existing	
Sound judgement						
thinks before acting						
thinks critically about television shows						
thinks logically						
finds out the facts before deciding reacts						
rationally instead of emotionally						
sets own priorities						
Responsibility						
accepts responsibility for own decisions						
does not offer excuses						
able to show hospitality						
cares for own belongings						
carries out allocated jobs around home						
gives good example to younger siblings						
Self-control						
controls appetite for food and drink						
controls impatience and temper						
controls imagination and curiosity						
manages own timetable						
easily able to accept difficulties cheerfully						
manages money and possessions sensibly						
able to detach from entertainment easily						
Courage						
bounces back after setbacks						
accepts correction						
physically strong, tough and resilient						
shows determination in the face of difficulties						
shows self-confidence						
speaks up against injustice						

[P for C: 65]

Performing the Virtues

Family activity

'You can easily judge the character of a man by how he treats those who can do nothing for him.'
Johann Wolfgang von Goethe

Play charades with a difference. Prepare cards according to list below: the four cardinal virtues and the virtues linked to them. Draw a card from a hat and perform the virtue to your team (act out the whole idea or break the word into syllables and perform the parts). Two minute limit. Total up the time for each team after a number of rounds to discover the winner.

Prudence	Justice	Fortitude	Temperance
Seeks truth and reality	Respectful of all	Courageous	Self-control
Discerns good from bad	Responsible	Magnanimous	Detachment from things
Able to set goals	Compassionate	Patient	Cheerful
Sincere	Generous	Persevering	Sober
Flexible with respect to opinions	Attentive to others	Resilient	Pure of heart
Seeks advice	Obedient	Industrious	Modest
Reflective	Grateful	Orderly	Enthusiastic
Idealistic	Able to forgive without grudges	Persistent	Serene
Mindful of own feelings	Leads others	Calm	Mild
Humble	Empathetic	Determined	Moderate
Optimistic and hopeful	Diligent	Ambitious to do good	Able to temper curiosity
Confident	Courteous	Forthright	Capable of awe and wonder
Decisive	Spirit of service to others	Honourable	Detached from opinions
Wise	Kind to all	Daring	Possessing peace of heart

[P for C: 28]

Key Strategies for Teaching the Cardinal Virtues

Discuss with friends

> 'Most people are other people. Their thoughts are someone else's opinions, their lives are a mimicry, their passions a quotation.'
> **Oscar Wilde, *De Profundis***

Write the cardinal virtue at the top of each list.

Consider how much importance you give to each strategy in your own home.

Think of two more teaching strategies for each.

• Teach right and wrong. • Coach your child in goal setting. • Show that writing a list it is easier to prioritise goals. • Teach problem solving by staying calm and breaking down the challenge.	• Insist on kindness to all. • Find joy in people not in things. • Put others first even when you are tired. • Smile when you see your loved ones.	• Model patience. • Name your fears to better confront them. Correct calmly. • Develop consistent routines, clear expectations and timetables. • Have a timetable and job list.	• Be mindful of distractions and target them. • Fix your face to give better emotional example. • Don't let screens take precedence over conversation in the car or at the table.
1. 2. (Hint: Think of ways you teach children to think before acting.)	1. 2. (Hint: think of fostering the right reason to do things… for others.)	1. 2. (Hint: think of how you encourage sound work habits.)	1. 2. (Hint: think of the loves you want to pass on.)

[P for C: 65]

Unity of the Virtues

Reflect

'Knowledge which is divorced from justice, may be called cunning rather than wisdom.'
Cicero

Tick the boxes that you feel currently characterise your child. Write the umbrella cardinal virtue for those qualities to the right.

- Ability to manage impulsiveness
- Ability to shut out distractions
- Self-control of temper
- Joyful

_____

- Persistence
- Patience
- Industriousness
- Orderliness

_____

- Well-developed conscience
- Capacity to think clearly and objectively
- Capacity to set goals for self
- Sincerity

_____

- Generosity
- Deeply held care for others
- Well-developed sense of responsibility
- An affectionate nature

_____

In every one of our good and freely chosen actions each of the cardinal virtues is present. If we have habits of self-control, we can use our fortitude to pursue wise goals for action that are for our own good and the good of others.

Without self-control of our impulsive behaviours, and of our fears of obstacles or discomfort which are both essentially self-centred, we would still be unable to carry out actions which take others generously into account, even though we may be able to set goals for ourselves and sincerely wish to seek what is true.

In the developing character of your child, on which cardinal virtues do you need to most keep focused?

[P for C: 51]

Virtue in Action and Intention

Parent - child talk

'We should be inspired by people... who show that human beings can be kind, brave, generous, beautiful, strong – even in the most difficult circumstances.'
Rachel Corrie

Virtue is flexible. Courage or self-control, or a habit of putting others first easily transfers from one activity to another.

Think of these five scenarios where self-control can be practised by a ten-year-old.

Scenario	What can you say to your child to encourage both a loving intention and high-quality performance of the action itself?
Not getting distracted during homework	
Not raiding the chocolate biscuits	
Coming to dinner when called	
Leaving one's room tidy in the morning	
Not taking a shower longer than it needs to be	

[P for C: 74]

What are You Seeing?

Set some goals — Brainstorm

'The remembrance of the heart is better than the remembrance of the head.'
A Manx proverb

Remember that all of our actions need to be informed by the cardinal virtues. Justice is the very habit of making non selfish choices. Selfishness, focusing on one's own desires without considering whether they conflict with responsibilities to others, is always wrong.

What patterns of behaviour do you see in your son or daughter? What aspects of character do these reveal? (An example is completed in grey.)

Behaviour	Positive virtue on show	Virtue required
Always helps with a smile when asked	Generosity, obedience	
Leaves unwashed things on sink		Industriousness, concern for others

For example, consider eating, recreation and work habits, personal hygiene, and social behaviours. Pay particular attention to habits of straightforwardness and generosity.

[P for C: 135]

24 hours of Personalized Character Building

Are there any changes you would like to make, in your parenting or in your dedication to each other? Focus only on the last 24 hours in reflecting on these questions.

The list below presupposes all the fun, banter, and normal challenges of daily family life, but you may find, on reflection that areas to grow also stand out.

- ☐ How united have you been as a couple in the last 24 hours?
- ☐ Did you consciously think in terms of building good habits in your children?
  - Were you encouraging with respect to personal priorities for each child?
  - Did anything in relation to the children in the past 24 hours surprise you?
  - Did you talk personally 1:1 with each child for any length of time?
  - Did you give your full attention when your child wanted to talk to you?
  - Are you conscious of changing any behaviour in order to give better example?
- ☐ Was there an opportunity to model and foster sound judgement?
- ☐ Did you do the thinking for your child?
- ☐ Did you ask your child's opinion?
- ☐ How did you model and teach sincerity?
  - Was there any moment where you felt the conversation was not totally sincere, in either yourself or your child?
  - Do you teach clearly what is right and wrong?
- ☐ Was there an opportunity to model and foster responsibility?
- ☐ Did you show affection for each child? Did you delegate jobs?
- ☐ Were there times when you were truly joyful, or at least with most evident peace of heart, in family interactions?
- ☐ Did you only correct your children lovingly?
  - Have you invested creativity in your family life in the past day?
  - How did you encourage a loving intention in the activities your child was doing?
  - How did you model and teach generosity?
  - How did you teach solidarity with those who are less fortunate?
  - Was there an opportunity to model and foster fortitude?
  - Did the both of you have consistent expectations?
  - Did you follow up the responsibilities that you had given to your child?
  - Did you keep to the family timetable, unless there was a good reason to vary it?
  - Did you take advantage of any crises to teach resilience?
  - Did you show any impatience?
- ☐ Was there an opportunity to model and foster self-control?
- ☐ Did you model a good self-restraint in relation to food and drink?
- ☐ Were there opportunities to teach detachment from material things?

[P for C: 14]

A Virtue Calendar

'Do small things with great love.'
Mother Teresa

Consider focusing on a virtue each month in the home. Rotate around the cardinal virtues every four months, putting an appropriate focus for the age of your child. Here is a suggested cycle.

	January to March	**April to June**	**July to September**	**October to December**
Cardinal virtue	Self-control	Fortitude	Respect and Responsibility	Sound Judgement
Some ideas for points to focus on 3-7.	• Stopping when asked. • Having to wait without complaining. • Create normal routine without treats.	• Not complaining. • Doing one's jobs. • Push their limits.	• Order: toys, timetable, etc, all out of love for family members. • Obedience.	• Telling the truth. • Learning to follow one's conscience.
7-12	• Sobriety and moderation… learning to stop oneself. • Not eating between organised meals and snacks.	• Cheer others up when things get difficult. • Fortitude to talk to others clearly but courteously.	• Kindness to all. • Generosity.	• Simplicity and directness. • Planning one's timetable. • Humility.
Teens	• Making sacrifices to achieve the goals one has set. • Recognise when emotions are in play.	• Constancy in pursuing challenging goals one has set	• Taking responsibility.	• Think first • Setting goals for oneself. • Loyalty to one's friends.

You may wish to tailor the calendar to other virtues of your choice.

[P for C: 34]

Sharpening the Virtue Focus

'We must never become too busy sawing to take time to sharpen the saw.'
Stephen Covey

Once you have a clear virtue focus for the weeks ahead...
- ☐ Launch the virtue each month in a special family meeting or dinner.
  - Elaborate the virtue. Decide on a slogan or a saying.
    - 'A place for everything and everything in its place'
    - 'Work before play'
    - 'One kind word can change someone's entire day'
    - 'Punctuality is about respect for others'
    - 'Wash the cup because you love the next person to use it'
    - 'There is more happiness in giving than taking'
    - I give others my full attention'
    - 'Self-control is the best superpower'
    - 'Trying again is the key to success'
    - 'Don't regret the goals you didn't set'
    - 'If you see a need act'
    - 'Never fear the truth'
  - Ask each child, and mum and dad too, to nominate a goal for the week focussing on the virtue. (Prepare a few suggestions beforehand.)
  - All share their goals and each week, review together over ice-cream in a family meeting.
  - Each month each take up another associated virtue or another angle on the same virtue, all under the same cardinal virtue.
  - Use it as a theme for one-to-one encouragement with each child.

- ☐ Lead by example. Make a resolution for yourself each week.
- ☐ Provide visual reinforcement of the month's saying prominently at home. Stick it on the fridge, stick it in the fridge. Put it up in different surprise places each week. Reward the first person to see it.
- ☐ Talk about the week's saying as a family. Change it up each week... be creative as a couple.
- ☐ Talk one-to-one with each child about the saying to help them see opportunities.
- ☐ Make Monday dinner an occasion to talk about the best successes you have seen in the week. Find something positive to say about each child's efforts.
- ☐ One-to-one chats in the car, or at bedtime.
- ☐ Give incentives when the resolutions are kept. Goals should be specific attainable and able to be evaluated.
- ☐ Read stories based from books such as *The Book of Virtues* by William J. Bennett.
- ☐ Even run a poster competition on a wet Sunday afternoon.
- ☐ Have your own reminders of the virtue on desk, dashboard, etc. Let the kids see that you have a specific goal each week. Help them set their own goal related to the saying. Be frank about your own resolutions to put the virtue into practice.

[P for C: 76]

New Year, New Goals

Parent-child talk

'The greater danger for most of us isn't that our aim is too high and miss it, but that it is too low and we reach it.'
Michelangelo

Do I set myself goals for personal improvement? Do I make resolutions each year for example? Do we set parenting goals for ourselves? Do I review these goals regularly?

Do I encourage my children to set their own goals for improvement also? Do I sit with them on the same side of the table when the school report comes so that they set their own goals?

Here is an approach. Help each child choose a goal for themselves within the four cardinal virtues and which will help their character make a big leap forward in one particular area. Try to ensure that the goals can be achieved in the year. Write the goal down so that you can keep it in mind.

And most important of all, have ongoing 1:1 chats during the year about your child's evaluation of their own progress. Remember these are not your goals, but your son's or daughter's goals. Ownership is everything. Offer your own encouragement and advice.

In the process set your own goals and think about sharing them with your child.

	Prudence	**Justice**	**Fortitude**	**Temperance**
Examples of goals... tie the idea down really concretely. The more specific the better.	• Learning to set oneself a daily goal • Asking advice. • Listening to others to learn something from everyone. • Honesty up front. • Confident in self without boasting.	• Speaking positively about others at the dinner table and in the car • Forgive others. • Offering to help. • Caring for one's friends. • Being grateful and cheerful. • Sharing.	• Doing one's jobs without being asked • Getting up on time. • Speaking up in class and overcoming shyness. • Tidying one's room daily. • Using time well on weekends and holidays.	• Doing homework without wandering around the house • Not eating between meals. • Managing one's temper. • Not complaining. • Learning to love reading.

[P for C: 16]

Mobile Creation

'Had we lived, I should have had a tale to tell of the hardihood, endurance, and courage of my companions which would have stirred the heart of every Englishman. These rough notes and our dead bodies must tell the tale.'
Captain Robert Falcon Scott

Make mobiles with your children... one major branch for each cardinal virtue. Hang them from the lights in your children's rooms. Talk about the virtues as you make the mobile. Think of a shape or a picture from a magazine to illustrate the virtue.

Alternatively:

- Find pictures in magazines that illustrate qualities of character.
- Google images of a famous person and make a mobile about that person, with different images expressing different qualities.

[P for C: 28]

Chapter 6

Chapter 7

SELF CONTROL

*'Most people are never happy and complain too much. It's too hot out, it's too cold out.
Life is beautiful. No need to complain so much.'*
Henry Flescher. Survivor of Dachau.

Discuss with friends

'Get off my worksite,' the builder roared at the two 15-year-olds who were skylarking on their first day of a service project in Wilcannia in the far west of NSW where they were supposed to be helping build houses for elderly indigenous parishioners. They were city boys in high spirits and in no frame of mind to nail themselves down to a morning of hard work as brickie's labourers. 'Go over there and sit in the gutter for the week.' They obeyed and plonked themselves down. The builder knew what would happen. He had a boy the same age. Ten minutes later one of the two came over, 'Please give us another chance.' He gave it to them, keeping his stern face. The two became his tireless assistants throughout the rest of the week.

What are the lessons from this? The goal of education is to empower young people with habits of self-management, so that they are free follow their own convictions about what is in fact and objectively good for them.

Self-control, otherwise known as temperance, is the habit of seeking pleasures appropriately... both exercising due moderation in pursuit of the enjoyments of life, and in learning to find pleasure above all in what is good, true, noble and beautiful. It is about finding joy in the right things, in whatever is good, true and beautiful. If we have acquired a love of order, of timetable, we will get more done. If we have acquired an openness to others, a readiness to appreciate others, and a love of family, we will be enriched by the joy flowing from these things. The benefits of self-control reach into every corner of life, from arriving home with a smile on our faces, to avoiding the triggers that can lead us into pornography. And sadly, when we are self-absorbed or when our desires are dominated self-indulgence, we become incapacitated in relationships.

Discuss with friends.

1. Self-control is about saying no to ourselves when we seek gratifications when they are not truly good for us: pleasures, possessions, power, rewards, comforts, etc. What are the most common areas where you see your child needs good habits in these areas?

2. More positively, temperance is the virtue of finding joy and delight in what is truly good for us? Where do you find yourselves 'reorienting' your child's attention from gratifications that may be too present in his or her life (fussy eating, comforts, individualistic enjoyments), towards gratifications that are more noble (delighting in conversation, getting outdoors, discovering knowledge, sharing music, having friends over, etc)?

[P for C: 58]

Practically Speaking

Prioritise

'(Children have become) canaries the coalmine of a sex-soaked culture.'
Miranda Devine

This table sets out some of the most obvious areas for growth associated with temperance. Talk together about how your son or daughter demonstrates with actions the qualities of self-control listed on the left. Tick the relevant boxes. For each of the 'Priority areas', write down in the 'Let's be specific' box a very specific moment you can take advantage of, or action you can take, to help your child develop the relevant habit.

Aspects of self-control	Current level of development					Priority areas	Let's be specific
	No evidence	Poor	Fair	Quite good	Well developed		
Controls appetite for food and drink							
Controls impatience and temper							
Able to control curiosity and imagination							
Manages own timetable							
Accepts 'no' and 'time to stop' cheerfully							
Thinks before acting							
Manages money sensibly							
Integrity and purity of heart							
Enthusiastic in doing good for others							
Joyful and light hearted							
Serene and mild							
Detached from entertainment							
Moderate. Does not need excess for enjoyment.							

Capable of wonder and awe							
Exhibits self-mastery							
Detached from material comforts for a good reason.							
Detached from possessions and gadgets							
Able to go without							
Does not complain							
Modest							
Appreciates beauty in nature							
A seeker of all that is good, true and beautiful							
Detached from own opinions							

[P for C: 58]

The Dimensions of Temperance

'Laugh a lot with your kids. Find the humour in their behaviour...Learn to laugh also at yourself.'
Ray Guarendi, Back to the Family

The Cardinal virtues are umbrella virtues. Each has a number of other virtues that shelter under it. By looking at these virtues we can gain a broader understanding of how the full spectrum of good habits associated with the cardinal virtue of temperance can be practised. Use the table to brainstorm some priorities for your parenting focus.

Virtues within Temperance	Relevant points of focus in your home.
Self-control	
Detachment from material things	
Cheerfulness	
Sobriety	
Purity of heart	
Modesty	
Enthusiasm	
Serenity	
Mildness	
Moderation	
Ability to temper one's own curiosity	
Capacity for awe and wonder	
Detachment from one's opinions	
Possession of peace of heart	

[P for C: 58]

Saying No to Oneself

Set some goals

There is a very famous experiment conducted almost 50 years ago by Walter Mischel, of Stanford University. Small children are given a marshmallow and promised a second in addition if they can leave the first uneaten for ten minutes. In the subsequent decades it became evident that the capacity for delayed gratification in this context was an effective predictor of academic, social, and moral success. Although each child starts temperamentally at a different base level, this type of affective education can be learned.

Affective education has as its goal the education of our desires and dispositions, so these become our allies in the many decisions we make each day that are good for us.

What are some opportunities to build the capacity in a child to delay gratification in the day-to-day life of a family?

List as many concrete examples as possible.

1. _____
2. _____
3. _____
4. _____
5. _____
6. _____
7. _____
8. _____
9. _____
10. _____
11. _____
12. _____

[P for C: 51]

A Self-Control Audit

Share from the heart

Heart to Heart

'It is the very pursuit of happiness that thwarts happiness.'
Viktor Frankl

	Does our child do his or her best …	Always	Often	Rarely	How can I help foster this virtue?
1	To control temper				
2	To manage impatience				
3	To overcome laziness				
4	To be kind to all				
5	In helping with jobs				
6	In cleaning up after self				
7	To hurry if asked				
8	To be cheerful				

[P for C: 86]

Stages of Obedience

Learning from others

'If children have learned to obey their parents, later they will be able to tell themselves what to do in the face of distractions and difficulties.'
Aristotle

Obedience is more than doing what we are told. It is the capacity to align one's own desires with those of another. It is the foundation for empathy, compassion and love. It requires humility and the capacity to subordinate one's own appetites and whims for a shared benefit with another person.

Much depends on raising children to be obedient: to parents, to God, and to their own conscience. If they prefer their own impulses to obeying their parents, when they are older they will have little capacity to bring their emotions under control. Children who have not learned obedience have been let down by their parents.

The best time for a child to learn obedience is younger not older. And the calmer the better. Angry and impatient instructions are more likely to teach fear and damage the parent child relationship, than teach obedience. Consequences for disobedience are best the direct result of the behaviour. Explain the link directly and simply. 'Because you didn't wait until your brother was served, you now have to go to the back of the queue.' 'Because you disappeared when mum asked you to wash up, you'll need to do that job each day for a week.'

Most important of all let us link obedience to love. Don't say: 'Do this because I said so!' Rather: 'Do this because it will help mum.'

And we adults need to model obedience: giving the example of being quick to anticipate the needs of one's better half. 'Your wish is my command.'

Maria Montessori describes the stages of learning obedience as follows:

- Age 3 and under: 'What we call the first level of obedience is that in which the child can obey, but not always. It is a period in which obedience and disobedience seem to be combined…. Even after three, the little child, must have developed certain qualities before he is able to obey. He cannot, all of a sudden, act in conformity with another person's will, nor can he grasp, from one day to the next, the reason for doing what we require of him.'
- 'The second level is when the child can always obey, or rather, when there are no longer any obstacles deriving from his lack of control. His powers are now consolidated and can be directed not only by his own will, but by the will of another.'
- The third level of obedience is when the child 'responds promptly and with enthusiasm and as he perfects himself in the exercise, he finds happiness in being able to obey.'

At what stage is your child?

[P for C: 58]

Are You Consistent As Parents in Your Expectations of Your Child When You See Your Child Acting Impulsively?

Take the test — Brainstorm

'Do not a allow a child to throw tantrums. Freedom that is unrestrained, results in a character that is unbearable. Yet realise that total restriction leads to a servile character.'
Seneca

The first step is always to audit our own example. We can't teach what we don't resolutely try to practise. Can you tick these boxes:

- ☐ I know how to say 'no' to myself. By coming to meals on time. By not taking calls that interrupt. By not seeking distractions in my work. By not giving in to saying a sharp word, or having the last word. By cleaning up after I finish.
- ☐ I don't buy impulsively. My default is to ask a second opinion.
- ☐ No matter how strongly I may desire something, I test my desires against good reasons. I ask myself 'Is this good for me and for others?'.
- ☐ Knowing that anger destroys relationships, I work resolutely so that I eliminate anger from my character?
- ☐ I don't give into idle curiosity. By gossip. On the Net. By participating in conversations that pry into matters that don't concern me.
- ☐ When I say 'no' to my children it is in order to teach them an important lesson. I give them reasons calmly and briefly. I try not react impatiently or critically. I know that children will learn to obey their own reason if they have learned first to obey their parents' reason.
- ☐ I try never to talk bitterly about others. I criticise behaviours not people.
- ☐ I am wary of becoming jealous of the possessions or popularity of others.

Teaching self-control to a child has two aspects:

- Training, from when child is very young, to obey reasonable requests and expectations. Consistency is essential to build up a habit. If a child has learned obedience when small, accepting reasonable requests in teenage years will normally not be a big problem.
- Educating a child with the good reasons they will need so they can tell themselves what to do. As a child grows towards adolescence, giving good reasons without entering into arguments is a crucial part of teaching.

The first of these requires great consistency.

Rank the consistency of your directions and guidance for your child, on a scale of 1 (least) to 5 (most). Then discuss and note reasons for inconsistency (eg parents' different standards, expectations too vague, our poor example) so that you can set goals for your parenting. Think about other behaviours of your child that cause you some grief and consider the reasons. For a very small child tailor your expectations accordingly.

	Activity	Least > Most Consistency					Reason for inconsistency
		1	2	3	4	5	
1	Getting up on time						
2	Snacking whenever						
3	Leaving rooms messy						
4	Coming to meals when called						
5	Putting clothes away						
6	Doing jobs on a roster						
7	Leaving bathroom respectable						
8	Looking after belongings						
9	Being fussy						
10	Going to bed						
11							
12							
13							
14							
15							

[P for C: 14]

Fostering Self-Control

Case study

'The essential achievement of the will is to hold one thought/attend to one object and hold it clear and strong before the mind, letting all others – its rivals for attention and all subsequent action – fade.'
William James

Invite some friends for supper and use this case study as a discussion starter.

All similarities to persons living or dead are purely coincidental.

> Waif is in Year 7. Her teacher feels she is quite intelligent and very immature. 'She strikes me as a girl who has never had much asked of her,' one said at a pastoral care meeting. Unfortunately, a month ago, Waif was in trouble at school and was suspended for three days. Her parents were called up to see the Deputy because she was had sent a graphic selfie to another student. Her mother looked upset and the father insisted that she should have her phone taken away. Four weeks on, she has been seen again with the phone causing the Deputy to contact the father. The father said, 'Yes I took it off her for a month, and she has promised not to misuse it again.' The Deputy explains that he feels it is unlikely the negative behaviours just go away. There is an awkward silence.

1. What do you think is the Deputy's concern? Do you agree with this?

2. How could this conversation be progressed in a constructive direction?

3. Can you see a way that the school can assist in giving Waif the help she probably needs?

[P for C: 141]

Learning to Pay Attention

Case study

'Finally, beloved, whatever is true, whatever is honourable, whatever is just, whatever is pure, whatever is pleasing, whatever is commendable, if there is any excellence and if there is anything worthy of praise, think about these things.'
Philippians 4:8

Let us develop the habit of paying attention as we choose, learning to fix our attention intentionally, not on impulse, not what is simply enjoyable or gratifying. The things we look at and think about are things we value. And what we value tells us a great deal about who we are. Those things that occupy our minds are the raw material of our needs and desires. A little mindfulness goes a long way.

Do I teach my children the importance of managing their attention? Do I know what my children look at, talk about, and look forward to?

Invite some friends for supper and use this case study as a discussion starter.

> Goldie is in Year 3. Her class teacher, Claire notices that she loses interest in the tasks she has to do and often has to be asked to refocus. Usually when corrected she gives a beautiful smile but then not much changes. She loves drawing and tends to practise this as often as possible, in most classes. The classmates at her table like her but she doesn't seem to contribute much when there are group tasks. She often forgets er readers at home, and sometimes also her runners for sport. Her teacher wants to help her be more responsible but is unsure where to start.

1. What character strengths would Goldie benefit from developing?

2. Give Claire some suggestions to help Goldie.

3. What suggestions could Claire offer to Goldie's parents?

[P for C: 131]

Reinforcing Positive Behaviours

Heart to Heart

'A thimble of honey is more attractive than a barrel of vinegar.'
Cardinal George Pell

Do you take a positive approach? Do you acknowledge and reinforce the positive behaviours?

What is your plan to build self-control? Think how you can model the behaviour you are encouraging. Think how you can help your child have ownership of their behaviour. Remember at the same time to foster a loving intention for specific behaviours.

We would like your child to grow in self-control in the following areas...	Ways that we will encourage and positively reinforce these behaviours
	a. b. c.
	a. b. c.
	a. b. c.
	a. b. c.

Ask further suggestions from friends.

[P for C: 70]

Too Much of a Good Thing

Heart to Heart

'Never go to excess, but let moderation be your guide.'
Cicero

The virtue of moderation is present when intentional choices moderate our desires.

As always, let's first think about our own example where the best motive for moderation is care for others. Tick these boxes:

- ☐ I focus on others in doing things I like. I choose recreations that help me be best parent, spouse, and friend that I can be.
- ☐ I know when to stop before I find myself eating or drinking, or even speaking, too much. I want to be at my best for others.
- ☐ I try to build these good choices into automatic habits: to get up when the alarm goes, to be first to get up when the doorbell rings, to get up from the table for something my spouse needs, etc.
- ☐ Even if a clear conversation is needed, I don't allow my words to wound. I say things in the most gracious way, without criticising the person.
- ☐ I don't resent being interrupted by my spouse or my children, or by anyone for that matter!

What are the things your child really likes doing? Think of the best reasons, that help others, to help your child practise the virtue of moderation. The first is done as an example.

Activity my son or daughter really likes	Best reason to moderate it on one's own initiative.
Playing Sonic the Hedgehog before dinner.	Stop when asked because mum has gone to a great deal of effort to prepare dinner.

[P for C: 146]

Are We Attached to Things?

'Care clings to our wealth; the thirst for more grows as our fortunes grow.'
Horace

Can you tick these boxes?

- ☐ Do we use material things to do good?
- ☐ Do we teach children that people are always more important than things?
- ☐ Parents mar the growth of generosity in children when they talk too much about their own 'toys' and purchases, and when they spoil children. Do we help children not to put their hearts in things?
- ☐ Do we avoid expensive presents which create the illusion that the more one possesses, the happier one becomes? It is not enough that children earn their money, we must ensure they don't think things will bring lasting happiness.
- ☐ Do we teach solidarity, the duty to assist people in serious material need? If we see a need we should act.
- ☐ Do we teach that the great sadnesses of life are not material deprivations, terrible though they are, but spiritual deprivations which are soul destroying? An absence of love and hope in a world of hatred and despair is even more terrible than a world of insufficiency.
- ☐ Do we foster habits of detachment: 'We use things but we don't put our hearts in them?'
- ☐ Do we go without things we don't need, or do we create needs for ourselves?
- ☐ Do we delay gratification? Do we ourselves wait with patience for things, putting off some purchases? Do we have the patience to wait for rewards?

[P for C: 102]

Buying Time... but the Clock is Ticking

Discuss with friends

'Banish indecent speech, and indecent pictures and speech from the stage, from the sight and hearing of the young. ... (until) education will have armed them against the evil influences of such representations.'
Aristotle

What would Aristotle have to say about unfiltered access to the internet for young children, or about giving a net-enabled smart phone to a child without ensuring first that this adult-in-the-making has the good habits and sincerity to avoid putrid websites.

A large cross parliamentary survey for the UK parliament in 2012 found that four out of five 16-year-olds accessed pornographic and potentially life-scarring material regularly, yet diligent parenting could have done so much to help them avoid these commercially created cesspits. Would it be any better now?

Protecting children is only the first step, diligent parents are buying time to form their character, and to pass on our most cherished values and faith.

How successfully are you protecting your child from negative influences in the years of childhood and early adolescence?

In the time you have bought, are you teaching skills of self-management?

[P for C: 150]

Shields Up Scotty!

'If love is not tied to truth, it falls prey to fickle emotions and cannot stand the test of time. True love, on the other hand, unifies all the elements of our person and becomes a new light pointing the way to a great and fulfilled life.'
Pope Francis

Are you protecting your child and using this safe space to educate them in trusting conversations? Sit together with your spouse and, for these twenty questions, score your parenting from 0 (absolutely woeful) to 5 (best practice).

____ Do you stay focused on the greatest task of parenting: to raise children so that they learn gradually to give themselves to God and others in loving affection and service? Nothing is more important in your life mission.

____ Is your family life habitually joyful and positive? Do you often invite friends to share the joy in your home? Do your children want to bring their friends home?

____ By your habitual delight in being with those you love, do you show that people are more important than things, and that reality always trumps the virtual world?

____ Are you coaching your child to be a 'soul of prayer' (St Josemaria), to have the habit of daily opening their heart to Our Lord about their life, their desires and experiences? Do your children see you invest 20 mins in prayer daily? Only in this way will they grow to look with God's eyes at reality and at their own situations.

____ Is your home a completely safe space for children? You are buying time so that you can personally form their hearts and minds. Are the screens in places where you easily can supervise? Are you diligent in strictly limiting social media for children and younger teens, giving the reasons why you do this? Do you limit gaming time carefully?

____ Are you close? Do you and your child have a relaxed trusting talk at least weekly? Does your child completely open his or her heart to you about everything in their lives? Do you diligently form the desires and the conscience of your child? Are your ongoing discussions with them about the facts of life and love, well ahead of every other influence?

____ Do you talk clearly with your son or daughter about how to protect themselves from the freely available dangers on the net? Do they trust you to talk about what they encounter on the net and in conversations with others? Do you know what they do online because they tell you.

____ Do you invest creativity in family life, planning enjoyable times together every week, without being dependent on screens?

____ Do you gently insist that in a family nobody should isolate themselves behind closed doors? It is a fine balance between respecting the privacy and personal space of a growing child, and naïvely allowing others to damage or even corrupt an innocent child's psyche.

____ Do you teach that time is a gift from God, not to be frittered away, and that the best recreations are doubly enjoyable because they are with others?

____ Do you avoid allowing your child a smart phone before you are totally assured that it will not damage them, and will not put undue pressure on other families? Do you help your child to see that the only effective way to prepare for future smart phone use is to have a well-formed conscience, to have mastered impulsive behaviours, to have high personal standards for purity of heart, and to be open to being guided?

____ Do you talk openly about video and movie choices, giving children criteria? Do you explain that we are diminished when we view obscenity and gratuitous violence and we cannot be accomplices to the abuse of others? Do you talk about how inappropriate scenes and images will stay in our minds a long time and dominate our imaginations? We must learn to be masters of our attention.

____ Do you use family meetings or one on one chats to plan screen viewing? Do you sit together to watch any material that may be problematic?

____ How do you fortify your child so he or she does not naïvely wander into inappropriate situations for which they are not ready, online or face-to-face? Do you talk together trustingly about peer group, the social world, social media coercion, and drugs?

____ Do you talk about the manipulative marketing agendas of pulp fiction, glossy magazines, and gutter talk on late night radio?

____ Have you implemented safe settings on game consoles, social media platforms, YouTube, etc? Is your home computer filtered?

____ Do you address any small instances of insincerity or deception, not by reacting in anger, but talking heart to heart?

____ Do you find yourself giving in to pestering? Are you awake to the danger of putting inexperienced children and teens on a pedestal as if they can do no wrong, and then finding it impossible to say no on important issues?

____ Do you create many family-based opportunities for your children to socialize? Or do you allow the poor example we see around us enter our own lives?

____ Before these things become emotional issues, do you talk trustingly and with much love about decency and modesty in clothing, and about family expectations for parties and friendships, that teenage years are a time for getting to know many persons of the opposite sex, but that early and mid-teen years are not the time for going steady?

____ Do you talk openly about the great importance of purity and prudence in social life? Do you talk to your teenage child about what to look for the father or mother of their future children?

Total _____

A score above 80% means you are safe from the Klingons!

[P for C: 139]

Sex Education: Think Through These Questions

Parent-child talk

'Lack of self-control betrays a fundamental defect in one's mind and reason.'
Cicero

Sex education is much more than biology. Biology can only capture the one aspect of human fulfilment in loving relationships. Parents are best placed to teach the full story, to prepare a child for mutually committed dedication. To be able to love in this way, he or she will need to have learned to give of themselves in small and in great ways without keeping tallies. No science class can teach this.

How effective is the education in sex and human love that you are providing? Discuss and tick them off.

- Have you laid foundations before emotions and peer group cloud the discussion? Do you talk clearly with your child in the years immediately before puberty? By age 10 a child should have received in loving conversations with his or her parents a complete under standing of the 'facts of life'. And then after that, ongoing, inspiring, clear guidance in human love and relationships. Do you present honest ongoing education in human love in all its dimensions, not reducing sex to the biological?
- Do you protect your pre-adolescent child from negative and harmful images, talk, and situations?
- Do you open your heart to your child? Do you explain the dangers of pornography, unbridled curiosity, masturbation, and all self-centred sexual behaviours, explaining that many in our society will not accept this view but that you want to guard those you love from the destructive self-indulgence that follows.
- Do you have frequent open-hearted discussions so that over time, every question or concern can be addressed?
- Do you talk clearly and energetically about the beauty of holy purity, about having a pure heart in a relationship, and of loving the whole person?
- Are you fostering the capacity for your children to think for themselves, looking objectively at issues and understanding the way their own passions and emotions work?
- Do you have close relationships with other families to provide a large 'extended family' where your teenager's social life can flourish and where they receive example of loving family life? The most natural place for social life to develop is in families and in homes.
- Do you create an extended social life that helps your child get to know many boys and girls their own age, and enjoy their company? Do you talk, well before it becomes an emotional issue, that pairing off with one girlfriend/boyfriend is not sensible or helpful in school years when the goal of social life is to mix around, no matter what Netflix promotes as normal.
- Does your child open his or her heart to you? (You cannot force this.)
- Do you build a lively and attractive family culture - the way we do things in our family, the way we talk, the respect we have for others, etc.

What can you improve?

_____

_____

[P for C: 149]

At the Neural Level: Temperance

Learning from others

'Some covered their eyes; some put their heads down and tried to go to sleep; some turned their back on the marshmallow; others played games with their hands; still others talked or sang to themselves about the second marshmallow that would get if they waited just a little bit longer. These 4-year-olds were able to wait–to control their desire for the marshmallow in front of them in order to double their reward–by using resourceful ways of tapping into the regulatory power of their upper brain.'

Psychologist Thomas Lickona discusses the capacity for four year olds to delay gratification

At the neural level, temperance refers to the healthy conditioning in our expectations for sense-based rewards. It refers to the reinforcement of neural reward systems so that they are activated either in response to, or in anticipation of, things that are truly good for us. Those expectations may be conditionings for certain preferences and behaviours by our upbringing. For example, we may have been raised in a family where we were taught not to keep others waiting, or to get up when we are called, or tidy up our own mess. Sometimes too we come to these qualities of self-management after childhood; they may be features of our character that we have established and consolidated by our own choices. For example, we may have trained ourselves to walk in the door in an upbeat cheerful mood when we arrive home.

Repeated experiences build up a reward expectation for better or for worse. Expectations are intensely motivating but they can bring unhappiness when the outcome was actually not good for us (eg a habit of viewing pornography, of eating junk food, of hitting the snooze button)? One way of viewing character formation is the need to 'program' healthy positive expectations... that we learn to look forward to things that are good for us.

1. What are positive and healthy expectations that we should 'condition' ourselves to look forward to?

2. What are positive and healthy expectations that we should 'condition' a child in our care to look forward to?

3. What (or better 'who') should we teach children to pay attention to?

4. What are three make-or-break areas where parents must show habitual joy, knowing that children will love what we love?

Chapter 7

Chapter 8

FORTITUDE

'Being deeply loved by someone gives you strength, while loving someone deeply gives you courage.'
Lao Tzu

James Mawdsley is the bravest man I have ever met. He described his prison ordeals in *The Heart Must Break: The Fight for Democracy and Truth in Burma* - horrific beatings, a broken nose, solitary confinement, intimidation and hunger.

I met him through his first cousin, Redfield's first school captain. As a university student in the 1990s James had backpacked into Asia but was appalled when the Thai border refugee camp, where he had made so many Burmese friends, was attacked and burned by Burmese troops sent by the military junta. He did the only thing he could think of... he went across the border and protested in Burma. He was deported within hours.

But the second time he did this, he was sentenced to five years in prison and tortured before being again being tossed out of the country after a month. During that month he came back to his Catholic faith.

He returned a third time, convinced that the world had a duty to know. He had pre-organised. Within three days he was sentenced to 17 years in prison. After a year, all the international outcry, diplomatic pressure, Time Magazine, speeches in UK parliament and in the UN, had put so much pressure on the junta that they took James to the airport in Rangoon and put paper in front of him to sign that he would never return to Burma. He said, 'I'm not signing anything. Take me back to prison.' They cut their loses and could not put him on the plane fast enough.

From prison he had written to his family:

> *God showers me with more blessings than I can count.... I ever remember Romans 5: 3-5 .... I have nothing whatsoever in the slightest to fear from man....Such limited opportunity for communication makes this abundantly clear: that love is all that matters, that it enjoys all things, that he trusts and rejoices in giving. I have so many to tell that I love them, that they have saved my life just by being there to be loved – but a single letter don't (sic) hold space for all your names. So I thank God for you in my prayers, and I thank him several times daily for the exact situation I am in – I am tumbling into Great Love with his Reality, with how things really are ordered. There is wickedness and suffering and hate, but what a joy it is to be a participant in their demise. I know this: that God (or Truth or Love or Good or Justice) has overcome.... I am full of hope.*

Once back in England, he was interviewed by David Frost and ran for parliament. Now he is a Catholic priest.

Courage is not about having the loudest war cry, but rather about self management in the service of what is right. The right management of one's fear and discouragement is at the heart of the virtue. For James, the virtue of fortitude was his considered readiness to put his life on the line for a good cause. For most of us, it is the habit of not losing our composure or peace of heart when there are difficulties. We teach fortitude by trying not to complain and by keeping a smile when we are tired.

Together, self control and fortitude are the habitual conditionings we need to overcome impulsive urges for gratification or to avoid discomfort. If we can manage the small daily challenges of managing our impulses of anger, vanity, overeating, etc, we will be better able to handle tougher external challenges, empowered by habits of fortitude. Most importantly self control and fortitude enable us to devote ourselves to those we love, and to ideals that serve our fellow human beings.

Discuss with friends.

1. Fortitude is about gritting our teeth when we have difficult challenges: staying optimistic, patient, improving in a subject, helping at home, working to a plan, having a timetable, etc. What are the most common areas where you see your child needs good habits in these areas?

2. More positively, fortitude is having the wherewithal to pursue great goals and to help others despite the cost. How can parents foster these ideals in a young person?

[P for C: 60]

Practically Speaking

'How can we expect righteousness to prevail when there is hardly anyone ready to give himself up individually to a righteous cause.'
Sophie Scholl

This table sets out some of the most obvious areas for growth associated with fortitude.

Talk together about how your son or daughter demonstrates with actions the qualities of fortitude listed on the left. Tick the relevant boxes. For each of the 'Priority areas', write down in the 'Let's be specific' box a very specific moment you can take advantage of, or action you can take, to help your child develop the relevant habit.

Qualities of Fortitude	Current level of development					Priority areas	Let's be specific
	No evidence	Poor	Fair	Quite good	Well developed		
Bounces back after setbacks							
Accepts correction							
Physically strong, tough and resilient							
Shows determination in the face of challenges							
Shows self confidence							
Speaks up in the face of injustice							
Calm. Not prone to anger.							
Patient							
Resilient not anxious							
Orderly							
Persevering and persistent							
Ambitious to be better							
Courageous							
Demonstrates a growth mindset							

Conscientious							
Gives leadership when it will help others							
Not afraid to speak up							
Capable of heroic self-sacrifice							
Honours commitments							
Able to ask for assistance							
Industrious and professional							
Uses time well							
Magnanimous							

[P for C: 60]

The Dimensions of Fortitude

'...Throughout the campaign he has led his men on all occasions with courage, cheerfulness, calmness and skill.'
Lt Col Ralph Honner, *Citation for Military Cross*

Brainstorm some priorities for your parenting focus if you are to raise a child with the full spectrum of good habits associated with the cardinal virtue of fortitude.

Virtues within Fortitude	Relevant points of focus in your home.
Courage	
Magnanimity	
Patience	
Perseverance	
Resilience	
Industriousness	
Order	
Persistence	
Calmness	
Determination	
Ambition to do good	
Forthrightness	
Sense of honour	
Daring	

[P for C: 60]

Fortitude is the Capacity to Manage Fears When it is Necessary to do so

Discuss with friends

'Be not afraid. Peace of heart is the great gift to those who know themselves to be children of God. Offer up pains. Fear only sin!'
St Josemaria

Which of these fears do you see in your child?	When?	Strategy to help overcome this fear (encouragement, baby steps, name the fear, example, etc)
Fear of a parent		
Fear of failure		
Fear of speaking in public		
Fear of the dark		
Fear of being alone		
Fear of being left out		
Fear of not meeting other's standards		
Fear of physical hurt		
Superstition		
Fear of strangers		
Fear of new experiences and the unknown		
Fear of particular animals		
Fear of scary sights		
Fear of criticism		
Fear of not being noticed		
Perfectionism		
Fear of punishment		

[P for C: 156]

Feelings Need to be Guided

'I can't expect my child not to run on feelings if for the whole ten to twelve years of his school life that's the example I have shown him in my behaviour.'
One parent's reflection

Normally our actions are motivated by something we believe is good for us. Our feelings, convictions, and objective reality should agree about what is best for us, but sometimes this is not the case. Feelings may not be good guides. Feelings can end up creating their own reality, for example when we overeat, when we give into impatience, when we don't confront a situation that needs confronting. Three big bowls of ice cream at one sitting may taste good, but they will not be objectively good either for a ten-year-old, or a forty-year-old.

Irrational fears or a disproportionate love of comfort too easily hold us back. Giving in to exasperation or to laziness also brings baggage into our lives.

Do I coach my son or daughter to overcome timidity as well as the impulsive pursuit of gratification? Do I encourage them to speak up in public? To ask questions in class? To organise things? To think big? To conquer their fear of discomfort that will stop them achieving anything worthwhile.

Which of these categories seem to describe your child? Taken too far, each approach can lead to incorrect choices. For the categories that may apply to your child, consider the possible dangers. The first is done as an example.

Disposition in the child	Possible danger if taken too far
A desire to keep peace at any cost	Dodges difficult issues.
A desire to avoid conflict	
A desire to please	
A capacity for empathizing	
Energetic decisiveness	
Enthusiastic	
Vivid imagination	
Adventurous	
Confident and with great 'self-esteem'	
Tends to be optimistic and cheerful	
Tends to be negative and look on the bleak side	
Assertive and pushy	

[P for C: viii]

Brainstorming Timetable, Repetition, Chores and Consistent Expectations

Prioritise

Heart to Heart

'You shouldn't pay your kids for chores; doing so robs them of the opportunity to be a contributing family member and to develop the habit of helping.'
Thomas Lickona

Timetable, regular jobs, and consistent expectations provide and environment where children can by repetition, quickly build up habits of responsibility and attention to others. Children who are raised in chaos are denied the structure they need to grow in self-discipline. When a child obeys mum's schedule and fulfils the daily duties she gives, that child later will more easily be able to tell themselves what to do. Aristotle first spotted this: 'By obeying the reason of a parent, a child learns to obey their own reason.' The alternative is unbridled impulsivity; children become victims of their whims and feelings.

Discuss.

1. As a couple spend some time structuring the day of each of your children. Don't make it complicated. A few simple times that can frame everything else: snack and mealtimes, shower time, bedtime. A few simple jobs that can go on a whiteboard checklist.

2. Revisit in a week or two to see whether you were both consistent in helping small children keep to this plan, doing tasks with them, giving them clear directions with affection, etc.

[P for C: 70]

My Timetable

Family activity — Family Meeting

'...a wealth of data shows that when young people are given meaningful responsibility and contact with adults, they quickly rise to the challenge, and their inner adult appears.'
Robert Epstein. Former editor-in-chief, *Psychology Today*

Teach your child to take some responsibility for their timetable.

With friends compare notes on how you teach children to organize and take responsibility for their time in a gradual way.

- Model good use of time.
- When children are small teach them that a day has a structure, and that punctuality is a social duty.
- To create positive patterns of behaviour rather than one offs, offer small incentives to small children for repeated behaviours.
- Encourage children to make the most of their time, setting their own goals from childhood.
- Teach the skills of self-management of time: timetables, scheduled jobs.
- Teach a love of reading. Limit screen time... find alternatives.
- Teach children to be aware of where their time has gone.
- Teach children to be goal oriented, not task oriented... In other words, achieve your purpose, don't just put in the hours; for a student this means master the material.

Then have your child of five or six decorate a simple timetable. At seven they should be able to compose it and decorate it.

[P for C: 13]

Teaching Order

Rank yourself 0 (worst) to 5 (outstanding) for the following 20 questions.

____ Do you lead from the front, demanding more of yourself than others? Don't be OCD about order but do be orderly with flexibility. A child's sense of order usually seems to be closely linked to the example set in the home.

____ Do you teach that the best reason to be orderly is to show our love... by being on time, by dressing well, by keeping our things tidy?

____ Do you expect your child to be responsible for his or her own things from as early an age as possible? Make it easy for a young child to be orderly: shoe racks, shelves, crates for toys, etc. Ensure there actually is a place for everything. Ensure there is sufficient space and places for things to be stored. Think of labelling shelves etc. Show don't tell.

____ Do you show that order brings you joy? Do you try to make jobs fun? Do you teach the beauty of simplicity and tidiness? By doing the cleaning up with younger children they see your happiness and learn the joy that order brings. Give lots of positive encouragement.

____ Do you teach the science of order: reason managing things? Teach simple systems and organisation. Use of simple apps and organisers. Teach the link between order and maintenance so things do not break or wear out quickly. Teach a rudimentary understanding of classification and taxonomy: systematisation of knowledge helps us access it, see the connectionsand make best use of it.

____ Do you teach personal hygiene and health: cleanliness of hair, nails, changing socks, washing hands before eating or preparing food, keeping lenses of glasses clean?

____ Do you teach that timetables and routines enable us to be more effective? Teach kids to push their time to achieve more, sometimes to work to deadlines. Children who know how to push themselves will achieve so much more and have at least the wherewithal to deliver more in service of others.

____ Do you teach the importance of rules and laws in life. Teach Aristotle's dictum: 'Law is order, and good law is good order.'

____ Do you teach how to prioritise one's time and activities. 'If it isn't listed, it can't be prioritized.' Order requires time so we need to invest time to be orderly. Teach children to block in key priorities first... family jobs, prayer, helping mum, study, and then to pursue lesser priorities such as recreation. Teach planning ahead as a way of fitting in competing priorities. Teach: how we spend our days is, ultimately, how we spend our lives.

____ Do you ensure that the home culture is formative? 'We clean up immediately.' 'If someone needs a hand, we help.' 'Work before play.' 'We care for things whether we own them or not.' 'Order saves time.' 'A place for everything and everything in its place.' 'Start well organised.' 'We always do our best.' 'We show our love by care of details.' 'Families help each other.'

Total _____

If your total is >80 things are pretty well 'in place'.
If not take the quiz again in 6 months to see if you have improved.

[P for C: 28]

I Love My Job!

'If he is old enough to walk, he's old enough to vacuum.'
One wise mum's motto

First some points for reflection...

- Am I careful not to be sloppy around home or leave the 'heavy lifting' for my spouse? Is our home and garden orderly, bright, and cheerful?
- Do we tailor jobs to the age of the children, making them more challenging each year as the children grow older?
- Do we show on our faces that helping others in their jobs makes us happy? Am I a model of someone who loves his or her work, takes pride in it, and sees it as service to others?

Have you distributed these chores?

- take out the rubbish
- clean shoes
- make one's bed (and change sheets when necessary)
- stack and unstack dishwasher
- simple cooking tasks
- set and clear the table
- sweep the kitchen and dining room
- bring in the washing from the clothesline
- put your dirty clothes in the wash basket
- fold your clean clothes where they belong
- assist with washing the car
- assist with the gardening
- dust the furniture
- clean glass doors/windows
- mopping bathroom
- sweeping the porch
- watering the pot plants
- feeding the pets
- mowing the lawn
- checking the mailbox

What can you add?

- _____
- _____
- _____

[P for C: 92]

How Well Are We Teaching These Attitudes to Work?

Share from the heart

Heart to Heart

'You don't build self confidence by putting low hurdles but by doing challenging work.'
Prof Mike Sayler

Work skill	What are we doing to teach each of these work skills?
I give my best. I do not 'get things out of the way', take short cuts, fail to prepare adequately, let others do my work, 'borrow' other people's work, 'download' assignments rather than thinking, etc.	
I know how to concentrate... I do not need distractions and breaks. I don't need to listen to music while I work.	
I have a personal timetable.	
I know how to fulfil my complete job description. I don't just focus on the urgent things.	
I look after details in my work because it is a sign that I see work as service.	
I establish daily routines.	
I don't complain about work. Work is a privileged service to others.	
I am professional.	
I balance my work with other priorities: family meals and chores, religious commitments, friendships, care of relatives, etc.	

[P for C: 71]

Make a Maintenance Inventory

'Chores are routine but necessary tasks, such as washing the dishes or folding laundry. Research suggests there are benefits to including chores in a child's routine as early as age 3. Children who do chores may exhibit higher self-esteem, be more responsible, and be better equipped to deal with frustration, adversity, and delayed gratification. These skills can lead to greater success in school, work, and relationships.

Suggestions by age include:

- *2 to 3-year-olds can put toys and groceries away and dress themselves with help.*
- *4 to 5-year-olds can help feed pets, make their beds (maybe not perfectly), and help clear the table after dinner.*
- *6 to 7-year-olds can wipe tables and counters, put laundry away, and sweep floors.*
- *7 to 9-year-olds can load and unload the dishwasher, help with meal preparation, and pack their own lunch for school.*
- *10 to 11-year-olds can change their sheets, clean the kitchen or bathrooms, and do yard work.*
- *Those 12 and above can wash the car and help out with younger siblings. Teens can help with grocery shopping and running errands.'*

The American Academy of Child and Adolescent Psychiatry. Facts for families #125

Involve the kids in creating an inventory of things that need maintenance in the house, from plants, to fish, to cleaning cars and shoes, to oiling hinges, to weeding the garden bed. Brainstorm. Divvy up responsibilities. Try to ensure that mum and dad don't end up doing things that others can do. Establish standing responsibilities. Post the plan prominently and follow up diligently in the first weeks so the routines are established.

[P for C: 28]

Family History

Family activity

'Grandpa was out with his boys, your uncles, putting in fence posts, and they stopped to boil the billy. Your grandpa gets bitten on the thigh by a redback. His sons said to him, "Pa, we better get you back to the farmhouse." "Nah, we finish the job. I'll be fine." By the end of the day his thigh was immensely swollen from the bite. They got him home. He was in a lot of pain, but he didn't see any point in going to the doctor. He applied his usual remedy: rum with a dash of lemon and a teaspoon of sugar, and a lie down. In the morning he was right as rain.'

Family legends

Compile stories of everyday family heroism from the past: rising at 4am every day for the milking, sitting up all night with a sick child, grandparent working three jobs, etc.

Can you get grandpa talking about times when things were not so easy?

Have children divide up the responsibilities to interview older cousins and relatives. Some will be treasure troves.

At the right moment can you talk to your son or daughter about the selflessness of mothers who are expecting?

Identify the virtues that are exemplified and talk about them.

Brainstorm stories that you can bring into play. Remember: it's always better to praise the heroism of others, not one's own!

[P for C: 80]

Home Biographies Library

'The strengths that make up courage reflect the open-eyed exercise of will toward the worthy ends that are not certain of attainment. To qualify as courage such acts must be done in the face of strong adversity. This virtue is universally admired, and every culture has heroes who exemplify this virtue.'
Martin Seligman

Biographies and autobiographies can provide a wonderful insight into virtues and character in action. Usually it takes time to build up a library so keep an eye on the local second-hand book shop to see what you can gather in a very inexpensive way. Here are some titles to keep an eye out for. What others can you add?

Prudence	Justice	Fortitude	Temperance
• Anne Frank. *Diary*	• Corrie Ten Boom. *The Hiding Place*	• Paul Brickhill. *Reach for the Sky* (The Story of Douglas Bader)	• Nelson Mandela. *Long Walk to Freedom*
• Viktor Frankl. *Man's Search for Meaning*	• Malala Yousafzai's *I am Malala*	• Neil McDonald. *War Cameraman: The Story of Damien Parer*	• GK Chesterton *Francis of Assisi*
• Alice Von Hildebrand. *The Soul of a Lion* (The story of Dietrich Von Hildebrand)	• Immaculée Ilibagiza. *Forgiveness Makes You Free*		• Helen Keller. *The Story of My Life*
• Takashi Nagai. *The Bells of Nagasaki*	• Russell Braddon. *Cheshire VC* (The story of Leonard Cheshire)	• Gereon Goldmann. *In the Shadow of His Wings*	• Weary Dunlop. *The war diaries of Weary Dunlop*
• Catherine Hamlin. *The Hospital by the River*	• Henri Dunant. *A Memory of Solferino.*	• Laura Hillenbrand. *Unbroken.* (The story of Louis Zamberini)	• St Therese of Lisieux. *The Story of a Soul*
• Peter Brune. *We Band of Brothers* (The story of Ralph Honner).	• Albert Schweitzer autobiography.	• Tilar J. Mazzeo. *Irena's children* (The story of Irene Sendler)	• Eddie Jaku. *The Happiest Man on Earth*
	• Annette Eberly Dumbach and Jud Newborn. *Sophie Scholl and the White Rose*	• Arrian. *Life of Alexander the Great*	• Xenophon. *Anabasis.* (The March of the Ten Thousand)
		• Gerard B Wegemer *Thomas More: A Portrait of Courage*	

[P for C: 19]

What Will You Use Your Courage For?

Parent-child talk

'Lead don't follow and you'll never walk alone.'
Johno Johnson

Courage alone is not much good to us if we use it for self-indulgent behaviours. We must put our courage at the service of ideals and at the service of others.

We can all think of moments when we have needed to walk out, stand up for our faith or values, support someone being criticised, or speak up in a group. Silence can mean complicity. Do you teach your children the fortitude of leading others in service? Do you teach your children to put convictions over fear of criticism every time?

Seek out stories with your children about moral courage. Spend some time showing your son or daughter how to search for information on the net. (Tip: go over the ground first finding the best YouTube resources.)

Some people to start with:

- Socrates
- Alfred the Great
- Joan of Arc
- Helen Keller
- Gandhi
- Dag Hammarskjold
- Alexander Solzhenitsyn
- Martin Luther King Jnr
- Mother Teresa
- John Paul II
- Shabaz Bhatti

Take the research further. Learn winners of the Nobel Peace Prize. Research figures outstanding in their thirst for justice. Take your child to the Nobel Prize site (https://www.nobelprize.org/) and then follow up with some vision of the person if it exists on YouTube.

Have follow up discussions over the dinner table about the research. Talk with passion about their service to others.

Pose the question, 'What did this person use his or her courage for?

[P for C: 154]

Do You Guide a Small Child in Developing Resilience?*

Take the test

'Learned helplessness is the giving-up reaction, the quitting response that follows from the belief that whatever you do doesn't matter.'
Arnold Schwarzenegger

Scoring:

2 Always
1 Sometimes
0 Never

____ Do you model positivity? Even in difficult situations? Do you see a crisis as an opportunity to remedy a fault that was always present but now can be seen and addressed?

____ Are you ambitious to take on challenging tasks that serve others?

____ Do you encourage children to take feedback and correction as a positive? Do you lead by example seeking feedback? Do you avoid excuses or blaming others?

____ Do you have problem solving strategies when you are not sure? Do you ask advice? Do you ask questions? Do you break problems up into small chunks that can be resolved?

____ Do you teach a child to offer up difficulties, seeing the hand of God in unexpected setbacks?

____ Do you make the effort not to show your own moodiness?

____ Do you demonstrate how to handle uncomfortable issues calmly?

____ Are you resilient against discouragement facing your own failures or mistakes?

____ Do you avoid complaining?

____ Do you stride through difficulties, avoiding any catastrophising about negative outcomes?

____ Do you avoid hovering over your children, but allow them, whilst ensuring their safety, to negotiate difficulties?

____ Do you normally expect your small child to carry their own school bag?

____ Do you have your child do up their own shoelaces?

____ Do you expect your child to pick up their own clothes?

____ Do you expect your child to make their own bed?

____ Do you teach children not to complain about discomfort, temperature, having nothing to do?

____ Do you avoid giving to your child different food from the rest of the family at mealtimes?

____ Do you expect a child who is already at school to cut up their own dinner?

____ Is bedtime for your child predictable?

____ Do you allow only an hour of computer games or less during weekdays? Or a couple of hours on a weekend?

____ When your child is walking around like a sad sack do you encourage them to make the effort to

___ be cheerful for the sake of the rest of the family?
___ Do you avoid impulsive purchases?
___ Do you raise children not to access the fridge and pantry on whim?
___ Are you united as a couple so your child gets the same answer from you both?
___ Is it important for your child to greet and farewell visitors to your home?
___ Do you expect your child to keep commitments of team training and practice of instruments, and to participate in all class and school events?
___ Do you give pocket money and expect reciprocal responsibilities?
___ Do you avoid trips to school to take items your child has forgotten?
___ Is the air conditioner turned off when not really necessary?
___ Do you avoid interfering in school discipline matters?
___ Do you always expect courtesy and good manners in your child?
___ Does your child have a habit of showers that are not too long?
___ Do you change your expectations if a tantrum is coming?
___ Is the TV turned off when nobody is watching?
___ Do you teach your child to talk sociably rather than play games or listen to music when at the table or when in the car on short trips?
___ Is your child resilient against giving up on tasks and jobs?

Total_____

>60 you have good systems in place to raise a resilient child

* This exercise and the one following are inspired by Chris Tanna's 'Soft Serve Test' questionnaire for the parents of Redfield College.

[P for C: 12]

Do You Guide Your Older Child in Developing Resilience?

'I didn't tell my kids, "You have to play viola, and you have to play piano." They chose these things on their own, and I don't think we have to give kids every choice, but we do have to give them some choice because that autonomy is crucial for fostering passion.'
Angela Duckworth, *Grit*

Scoring:

2 Always
1 Sometimes
0 Never

____ Do your children see you set goals and stick to the plan to achieve them? For example, to paint the house, to learn a new skill, to plant a garden?

____ As a family do you persevere in prayer to help others?

____ Do you avoid boasting about your children?

____ Do you raise your child to speak up with boldness, honesty and constancy?

____ Do you commit yourselves to noble causes?

____ Do you coach your children to have the difficult conversations... eg with a teacher when home work has been forgotten, with another student who is doing something annoying?

____ Do you keep calm in the face of difficulties?

____ Do you avoid impatience? Do you correct children calmly?

____ Do your children sense your confidence in God our Father who brings good out of difficulties for those who know how to trust him (Romans 8:28)?

____ Do you have a character development goal for your child that you have discussed in the last day?

____ Do you bring joy and humour into the home every day?

____ Are you close enough for trusting conversation about any topic?

____ Are you focussing on fostering specific positive habits?

____ Do you address negative habits early? The earlier the better.

____ Do you teach children to break problems up into small chunks that can be resolved?

____ Do you say 'yes' to challenges? Do you give example in this?

____ Do you say 'no' essentially when it is a question of physical or moral danger?

____ Do you allow your child to make their own plans when there is no physical or moral danger?

____ Does your child readily accept your decisions?

____ Do you ensure that lazy habits do not get a foothold?

____ Is family life shared and lively or do family members isolate themselves?

____ Do you address poor sibling example early?

____ Do you set reasonable expectations for getting up time on weekends and in school holidays?

____ Are you comfortable in taking away a privilege that is misused?

____ Do you address habits in your child of allowing distractions and of wandering around while doing homework?

____ Do you have difficult conversations with affection?

____ Do you normally avoid material rewards?

____ Do you get out into nature for camping and bushwalks?

____ Do you give the example of being detached from technology?

____ Do you give all your attention when your child is talking to you?

____ Do you have community service initiatives as a family, often?

____ Are you creative in school holidays? Do you teach the value of time?

____ Do you help your child set goals in every dimension of their life: spiritual, physical, intellectual, social, academic?

____ Do you help your children to face the consequences of their decisions?

____ Do you help children learn from every small failure?

Total_____

>60 you have good systems in place to raise a resilient child.

[P for C: 91]

At the Neural Level: Fortitude

Learning from others

'Our kids simply don't know what an adult is—or how to become one. Many don't see a reason even to try.'
Ben Sasse, *The Vanishing American Adult*

At the neural level, fortitude is characterized by the development of pathways of cortical regulation of our fear responses and fearful and anxious memories. In essence it is a conditioning of our fear responses so that they are neither paralysing nor creating underperformance. This involves rich fear dampening connectivity between amygdala and specific areas of the prefrontal cortex, where we have the resources to assist in processing and managing our fears.

1. What are the joy-sapping fears that can easily condition the outlook of an adult in our society?

2. What are the make or break areas where you do not want fear of failure to take root in a child's psyche?

3. What are the make or break areas where you do not want fear of discomfort to take root in a child's psyche?

4. What are the make or break areas where you do not want fear of peer disapproval to take root in a child's psyche?

Chapter 9

JUSTICE... GIVING OTHERS WHAT IS THEIRS BY RIGHT

'Love does not dominate; it cultivates.'
Johann Wolfgang Von Goethe

Discuss with friends

Early one morning I received an urgent call from Fergus: 'I need to get Renee to the hospital, can you bring us?' Ten minutes later I pulled up outside his apartment and he carried his young semi-conscious wife down the steps to my car. Very chivalrous and very concerned. At the emergency centre of the largest hospital in the city, an attendant, protected from assault by security wires, talks to the obviously-dazed young woman: 'Name,... address,...Medicare details,... phone number,... date of birth.' Question after question.

By this stage Fergus is holding Renee up. All chairs are away from the counter and bolted to the floor. The attendant asks Renee to stretch her arm between the security wires to check her blood pressure, but her legs buckle and she faints. Fergus lifts her back to the seats and only then do they bring a wheelchair.

What's the point? The attendant was courteous and trying to help, but she was helping on her terms. Justice brings the obligation not just of doing something, but of doing all that is needed. We easily sell justice short... justice is much more than simply paying our taxes. It is in play in every interaction between persons.

Without justice, in families we serve others on our own terms. We love them on our own terms. We do not give of our very selves. Blessed Alvaro Del Portillo captured this idea, writing about the challenges faced by parents:

> *'The frantic pace of modern times does not seem to foster calm dedication to children. We have more and more of everything, except time for others. There is a risk that parents may be devoured by work, even though it is done for the sake of their children's future. But their future well-being depends a lot more on the time parents have generously given rather than on the material comfort provided. Children do not complain so much of not having been given this or that by their parents, as of parents who have not given themselves to the family.'*

There is no substitute for personal presence. Let us be truly dedicated to those we love by our presence, by keeping them in our thoughts, by praying about their deepest needs, and by serving them in our actions.

Discuss with friends.

1. Justice, on the one hand is composed of habits of universal respect and deep responsibility towards others. How can parents develop these qualities in a young person in their care?

2. More broadly, justice is the habit, in every single choice we make, of taking others into account. It is the starting point of love. It is the antidote to the self-centred goals, the self-indulgence, the self-affirmation and vanity, that children can so easily absorb from the media, from peers, and from us. Where can we ourselves give even better example of having the fundamental orientation to others that is at the basis of true love?

[P for C: 55]

Practically Speaking

This table sets out some of the most obvious areas for growth associated with justice. Talk together about how your son or daughter demonstrates with actions the qualities of justice listed on the left. Tick the relevant boxes. For each of the 'Priority areas', write down in the 'Let's be specific' box a moment you can take advantage of, or action you can take, to help your child develop the relevant habit.

Qualities of Justice	Current level of development					Priority areas	Let's be specific
	No evidence	Poor	Fair	Quite good	Well developed		
Always kind to others							
Accepts responsibility for own decisions							
Does not offer excuses							
Affectionate							
Always courteous							
Cares for own belongings							
Fulfils chores							
Always gives good example							
Obeys willingly and promptly							
Appreciates goodness							
Attentive and good listener							
Empathetic. Considerate for the feelings of others							
A good friend							
Thoughtful							
Reads social cues							
Understanding. Adapts to various personalities							
Grateful							
Forgiving							

Loyal. Faithful							
Fair							
Cooperative and easy to work with. Good in a team							
Compassionate							
Merciful							
Gives people more importance than things							
Sincere with others							
Trustworthy							
Generous and able to love with all one's heart							
Shows solidarity with those less fortunate							
Caring							
Honourable. Able to know one's duty and wanting to fulfil it							
Makes others feel appreciated							
Humble, without self-importance							
Light hearted							
Tolerant. Accepting and respectful of persons							
Diligent							
Strives to completely fulfil personal potential							
Patriotic							
Able to laugh at self.							
Hospitable							

[P for C: 55]

The Dimensions of Justice

One young couple spoke of how they took their young family of five children away on a tropical holiday. After fabulous weeks of new and costly experiences, the father asked the six-year-old, what she enjoyed most about the holiday. She replied, 'When we all held hands and jumped into the pool together'.

So simple. Dad now invests in daddy-daughter time, kayaking with his daughter on Saturday mornings.

Justice is the virtue that underpins relationships. It is the habit of always taking others into account, and the impact of our actions on them. It is a prerequisite to the love for others that must underpin every virtuous act. Responsibility is the virtue governing our duties to care for and dedicate ourselves to those we love, and to educate those in our care. In the professional environment, it means seeing our work as service and not simply as a means of personal affirmation or advancement, or material benefit. In any position of responsibility to others, this virtue leads us to deal with others respectfully and personally, never seeing them as means to an end. Through courtesy, kindness, and sincere service, both parties are enriched.

Brainstorm some priorities for your parenting focus if you are to raise a child with the full spectrum of good habits associated with the cardinal virtue of justice.

Virtue within Justice	Relevant points of focus in your home
Respectfulness of all	
Responsibility	
Compassion	
Generosity	
Attentiveness to others	
Obedience	
Gratitude	
Ability to forgive without grudges	
Capacity for leadership	
Empathy	
Diligence	
Courtesy	
Spirit of service	
Kindness to all	

[P for C: 57]

A Family is a Place Where We Help Each Other

Family meeting

'Never see a need without doing something about it.'
Mother Mary Mackillop

Use a family meeting to reflect more deeply on each other's needs.

The table below (with sample answers) may help in your planning and discussion. Each person can talk honestly about their own needs and then add suggestions. Dad should defend the principle that Mum should not do something that anyone else is capable of doing.

	Mum	**Dad**	**Mary**	**Peter**	**Grannie**
Moments when help would be much appreciated	'It would help me if whoever is home helps to bring the shopping in from the car.'	'It would help me if everyone was ready to leave at 8am each day, otherwise I'm late for work.'	'It would help me if there were no big distractions from music practice and gaming while I'm studying.'	'It would help me if I don't have extra jobs in the morning so I can do my music practice then.'	'It would help me if everybody dropped in to my flat for a quick hello each evening.'
Ways we can take some of the load off mum.		I'll coordinate the washing up.	I'll mop the bathrooms each week.	I'll get up when I'm called first time each morning.	

[P for C: 72]

Do I Focus My Attention on Others?

Reflect

'Men were brought into existence for the sake of others, that they might do one another good.'
Cicero

Can you tick each of these boxes?

- ☐ Love starts with paying attention to others, at being joyful when we see them, when they visit, when they talk to us. Does my face light up when I see my children or my spouse after a long day?
- ☐ Do I smile whenever I meet someone?
- ☐ Do I try to brighten up for the sake of others?
- ☐ Do I habitually give my attention to others by paying attention to them?
- ☐ Do I model empathy with others... are my emotions normally in sync with the person with whom I am talking?
- ☐ Do I know what is on the mind of each member of my family and do I pray for them and support them?
- ☐ Am I a good listener?
- ☐ Do I respect other's feelings, opinions, beliefs, and personal space?
- ☐ Do I make rash judgements about others? Do I follow the principle 'If you can't say something positive, say nothing'?
- ☐ Do I find something to admire in each person?
- ☐ Do I experience the joy that comes from seeing the good fortune of others?
- ☐ Do I always put people above things, delighting in people and not getting distracted by things?
- ☐ Do I strive to give good example always, everywhere?
- ☐ Do I organise family activities and activities that are positive and joyful?
- ☐ Do I teach my children to look forward selflessly?
- ☐ Am I a kind and considerate person?
- ☐ Do I ring others back promptly? Do I remember to ring them to wish them happy birthday?
- ☐ Do I pay carry out small hidden details of service?
- ☐ Do I keep others in my thoughts and prayers?
- ☐ Does my joy spring from my trust in God and gratitude?

[P for C: 147]

Tradition of Family Helping Each Week

Family activity

Family Meeting

'Serve one another through love'
Galatians 5:13

'Love your neighbour as yourself' means that in everything I must treat my neighbour as I would treat myself. If I feed myself, I have a duty to ensure my neighbour has food. If would defend myself, I have a duty to defend my neighbour, when he is vulnerable. Are you teaching this to your children?

Create a tradition that each week as a family we do something to help others outside the home. Take it in turns to nominate the task... the more creative, the more idealistic, the more compassionate, and the more fun, the better.

Some possibilities:

- Everyone makes cards for Grannie for Mother's Day.
- Help a neighbour move.
- Record a family message on an idealistic theme and send it to a politician or media.
- Organise a working bee in an elderly neighbour's yard.
- Clean the grandparents' windows.
- Run a family BBQ for a cousin's birthday.
- Set up a Saturday morning hot chocolate stall on a prominent corner to raise money for a charity.
- Visit to a nursing home as a family.

[P for C: 97]

Saying Thank You

'When it comes to life the critical thing is whether you take things for granted or take them with gratitude.'
G.K. Chesterton

Love is grateful.

Gratitude is such a fundamental virtue. We should not get ahead of ourselves. Humility makes gratitude possible. Do I teach children to be humbly grateful for all the good and beautiful things God has given us? Is 'Thank you' often on my lips in family life?

How is your example?

- ☐ Today I have thanked my spouse for some specific service or help.
- ☐ Today I have gone to some trouble to thank someone.
- ☐ I often send emails and cards showing gratitude for specific services I have received from others (cards take more effort and can be a sign of greater gratitude).
- ☐ I have often told my parents how grateful I am to them.
- ☐ Today I have thanked each of my children for some effort they have made.
- ☐ I am known as a grateful person in my workplace.
- ☐ I say thank you with a smile.
- ☐ I teach my child about to say thank you habitually, with examples.
- ☐ I say thank you every meal, and I never complain about food.
- ☐ I thank God at the end of every day.

Total ticks: _____

Draw your own conclusions about your score. Now share your results with your better half to seek objective input, and to ask reminders and encouragement to grow in the areas you need to improve in.

[P for C: 159]

Showing Thank You

Take the test — Brainstorm

'There is nothing I would not do for those who are really my friends. I have no notion of loving people by halves; it is not my nature.'
Jane Austen

Joy is a great motivator. Being conscious of the joy we feel predisposes us to repeat that behaviour in the future.

Do you help your child to learn joy and gratitude by your example?

Do you show thank you with your smile and good humour:

- ☐ When you sit down to a meal you did not prepare?
- ☐ When you are served in a shop?
- ☐ When there is a delivery to your door?
- ☐ When your clothes have been washed or ironed for you?
- ☐ When someone else has vacuumed your room?
- ☐ When someone picks you up in the car?
- ☐ When someone else brings the mail in, or puts the garbage out, or helps with the groceries?
- ☐ When someone is on time for you and does not make you wait?
- ☐ When someone makes the effort to dress well to show their courtesy or love?
- ☐ When someone comes immediately when you call?

Total ticks: _____

Draw your own conclusions about your score.

[P for C: 80]

Fostering Friendship

Case study — Discuss with Friends

'Study the welfare of others not your own.'
Philippians 2:3

Invite some friends for supper and use this case study as a discussion starter.

> It is a few months into Year 7. Millicent, a new girl, is in your daughter's English class. You hear she likes the subject and generally she is on top of her work, but she is very shy, and the class sees that she prefers to work alone. Your daughter says that Millicent looks sad on many days. She eats her lunch alone. Nobody dislikes her but she seems to have few friends. When you start chatting with Millicent's mother in the car park, the mother says abruptly and definitively, 'I always tell her not to have friends, they only let you down.'

1. How could you constructively progress this conversation? Can you suggest a line of action that may be acceptable to the mother?

2. How could you talk to your own daughter about helping Millicent and about the value of friendships?

[P for C: 98]

Teaching Generosity

Discuss with friends

'Generous people act unselfishly and cheerfully for the benefit of others, conscious of the value of their help and despite the fact that it may cost them an effort.'
David Isaacs

Generosity is the virtue underpinning the capacity to give ourselves in loving relationships to other people and to God.

Only true love, 'the gift of oneself' according to St John Paul II, fulfils the human heart.

Do I have well practised habits of helping friends and relatives even at the cost of great inconvenience? Do I put others first? Do I avoid taking the last piece of cake, the softest seat, the best place? Do I habitually make light of impositions on my own time and energy? Do I model service to others that springs from love not from obligation... from internal convictions of solidarity with those who need help, not from external impositions?

Generosity helps a teenager break out of the introspection of early adolescence. Generous ideals are an antidote to selfish material goals. The virtue of generosity prepares young people to do much good in their adult lives modelling their lives on the one who 'went about doing good'.

How is my example? Do I teach my child that things can wait? Do I demonstrate this by giving my full attention when someone is talking to me? Do I avoid interrupting meals, conversations, family time, or prayers when my mobile phone rings? Do I allow my own things to preoccupy my thoughts? Do I give my time generously to others?

Do I work side by side with my children? Do I give each child well-chosen jobs and help the child to see that each job as a way of helping others?

Here are ten ways to teach generosity. Talk together as couple about these and decide what works in your home. Then bring your best examples to your group of friends over coffee.

1. Teach by the example of how you and your spouse care for each other. With your spouse, model this secret ingredient of loving relationships. Help others cheerfully. Habitually make light of impositions on their own time and energy.
2. Give your time and attention to every family member without stint. Stop what you are doing to look at the person talking. Listen giving your full attention. If a person needs to talk more, listen more. Your example will be decisive.
3. Keep people's needs in mind. Ring your spouse to see how the day is going. Follow up issues so are doing what you can to help. Stay up to date. Ask how things are going.
4. Don't miss birthdays and anniversaries of old friends.
5. Guide your small child how to be generous with very specific instructions. Make suggestions to an older child, pointing out the good they will do and the joy they will bring, but leave them totally free.

6. Debrief when your child falls short. Teach your child to look at the causes of their own behaviour, and at the effect it had on others. Always show how uncharitable behaviour impacted on others. Go for the heart.
7. Have high expectations. Teach that jobs are service. Give children small well chosen jobs and help the child to see that this job is a way of helps others. To build generosity, of ten ask children to do deeds of service for *other* children in the family, for example, have children make each others' lunches.
8. Refine a generous home culture of smiling service to each other, hopping in to offer assistance, taking over when someone is tired, considerate phone calls when held up, keeping in touch during the day when a day is particularly tough.
9. Teach generosity by teaching detachment. 'We use things but we don't put our hearts in them.' Teach that happiness is in relationships not in things. Parents mar the growth of generosity when they talk too much about their own purchases, and when they spoil children. Avoid expensive presents creating the illusion that the more one possesses, the happier one becomes. It is not enough that children earn their money, foster habits of detachment.
10. Teach generosity by fostering solidarity with those who are less fortunate. Teach the crucial lesson of the happiness that comes from serving others. Talk about ideals around the dinner table. Children learn by watching – so 'bring them with you'. Work with your child in the service of others mowing the elderly neighbour's lawn, visiting grandparents more often, dropping everything to visit a friend who has suffered a misfortune, etc. Plan Sunday visits to nursing homes with your child. Reinforce the schools' community service program. Work with your teens in a soup kitchen on a Friday night.

What further ideas and suggestions can you put on the table?

[P for C: 97]

Mantras for Solidarity

Learning from others

'He who lives only for himself is truly dead to others.'
Publius Syrus

Use these mantras to build a home culture.

- *'In a family we help each other.'* A family, underpinned by mutual self-sacrifice, is the most natural place for a young person to learn solidarity with those in need. The motivation to help is love for others. In a family one normally helps, not because one expects a reward but because one perceives a need. Model service to others that springs from love not from obligation... from internal convictions of solidarity with those who need help, not from external impositions.
- *'There is more happiness in giving than in receiving.'* (Acts 20:35) Helping brings happiness. When our focus is on another's needs, it is much easier to forget about one's own complaints list. When we help others our peace of heart and happiness shows on our faces.
- *'When you see a need, act.'* Let us surround children with idealism. Conversation at the dinner table is powerful. Don't just rely on chance... bring topics occasionally. We must never forget those who are less fortunate. Compassion leads us to pay attention to the needs of others and to act.
- *'Happy family. Happy society.'* Let's raise children to understand that when families flourish, society flourishes. Find the right time to talk to children about domestic dysfunction and domestic violence, absent fathers, etc.
- *'What will you use your courage for?'* Let us teach responsibility for the society in which we are citizens. Let us foster big ideals of service in society, teaching children to be well informed and have the courage to speak up. We may encourage children to follow the political party of their choice and demonstrate how to be involved in debate on ethical issues... talk back, letter writing to media, politicians and parliamentary committees. Let us talk about our ideals with a passion.
- *'When we need help; just ask.'* In a family if we have a need, we are simple and direct. There is no room for shyness and wondering what others will think. There is no room for mockery and sarcasm. We pass on our advice with affection and then leave a child free to apply it without compulsion.
- *'In a family we share what we have, with family first and then with others.'* Teach the universal principles of social justice: respect for the human person, concern for the common good, solidarity, subsidiarity, participation, a conditional right to private property, and the 'option for the poor'. When we are generous, personal problems disappear. Can we mow the elderly neighbour's lawn, visit grandparents more often, drop everything to help a friend move, or visit a friend who has suffered a misfortune?

[P for C: 99]

Learning Social Skills

Case study

'Three things in human life are important. The first is to be kind. The second is to be kind. And the third is to be kind.'
Henry James

Invite some friends for supper and use this case study as a discussion starter.

All similarities to persons living or dead are purely coincidental.

> Brutus, in Year 5, is the oldest of three brothers. He is loud and a big personality, but not unpopular with both teachers and classmates. There doesn't seem to be a mean bone in his body, but whenever there is a disagreement in the class or a squabble in the playground, Brutus always seems to be involved. When he is in trouble he is truly repentant.

1. What character strengths would Brutus benefit from developing?

2. What strategies would you suggest that could help Brutus?

3. Offer some suggestions for his home life.

[P for C: 16]

Recycling Toys

Family activity

'The more we are concerned for the well-being of others, the closer we will feel to each other.'
Dalai Lama

Go to Vinnies or the Smith family, explain how the shop works and invite each of the children to choose a cheap toy and buy it for them. Explain that these things are all donated for others to use, and that the charity uses the money it makes to give food and support to the homeless and less advantaged. Explain that we will come back, and each donate a toy for others.

Make a specific day (the first day of Spring or the first Saturday of the summer holidays, for example) an annual event, with a family picnic to mark the successful clean out of cupboards of old clothes and unused toys, Tupperware, and tools. Take them to Vinnies on the way to the picnic. Make the donations. Even have each child hide a note in the toy they are giving away saying 'I hope you like this'. Don't give broken things away, throw them out. Make this a really cheerful day. Talk about the joy for the person who finds the toy in the shop.

[P for C: 102]

Are the Loving Motivations in Place?

Prioritise

Heart to Heart

QUALITY OF CHARACTER OR GOOD HABIT	A. Current level of development			B. Motivation			C. Priorities for the year
	Shows this quality readily	Sometimes apparent	Rarely demonstrated	Carries out these actions habitually out of love for others	Occasionally can act in this way out of love for others	Often carries out these actions for self-interested motives	Tick the boxes beside priority points of focus for individual child
Sound judgement							
flexibility							
understanding							
loyalty							
audacity							
humility							
optimism							
Responsibility							
obedience							
sincerity							
orderliness							
Self-control							
modesty							
moderation							
sociability							
friendship							
respect for others							
simplicity							
patriotism							
Fortitude							
perseverance							
industriousness							
patience							
responsibility							
justice							
generosity							

[P for C: 74]

Helping a Young Person Realise that Their Actions Impact on Others

Parent-child talk

Here we focus on equipping a child with true and good reasons so that later they can be self-directing. It's not effective in the long run to demand obedience and compliance... we are training children to run their own lives.

Remember that with a small child, it is less a matter of giving reasons, and more a matter of consistent training. But there comes a point where every child has to learn to guide himself or herself, knowing how much responsible actions communicate respect, gratitude, kindness, etc.

What reasons do you equip your child with? The best reasons normally focus on our responsibilities towards others. The first is an example:

Action	Best reason focusing on responsibility to others
Washing a cup instead of leaving it in the sink	'Wash the cup because you love the next person who will drink from it.' (Mother Theresa)
Getting up when called the first time	
Not leaving the table until the meal is finished	
Dressing with care	
Putting dirty clothes in the laundry basket	
Not helping oneself to the biggest piece of cake	
Claiming the best seat always	
Having to be called again and again for dinner	
Not turning off the game when asked	

[P for C: 104]

Chains of Events

Parent-child talk

'Service to others is the rent you pay for your room here on earth.'
Muhammad Ali

Create chains of events to make responsibility easier.

Compose it with the child. Ask them to write it down on a poster.

For example:

> 4pm arrive home
> Leave school bag at desk.
> Change.
> Dirty clothes in laundry.
> Help prepare afternoon tea for little brother.
> Share stories with mum.
> Clean up afternoon tea.
> Start homework.
> 20 minutes reading.
> 5 minute shower.
> Dinner.
> Sweep kitchen floor.
> Brush teeth.
> Say prayers.
> 8pm bed

[P for C: 72]

Teaching Children to Think About Society

Discuss with friends

Some who talk about building character make the mistake of just emphasizing moral reasoning, as if we could just think our way out of bad habits. But moral conclusions depend most of all on the capacity for positive moral feeling that motivates our behaviours. We learn by doing. Without compassion, kindness, empathy and responsibility, which are all dimensions of moral feeling, we will struggle to morally reason correctly.

Below are listed the foundational principles of harmonious society. How do you ensure that your child takes this great heritage of mankind to heart?

Use the following table as a planning template. This will pay off handsomely in the life of your child.

Remember passionate example is crucial. Children need to see us take action when something is wrong. They need to see us react: writing to the TV channel, making an appointment with a parliamentarian, contacting the media, joining a political party?

Be creative and be impassioned.

Principle of social ethics	Conversations and stories by which we can communicate these principles.	Experiences that will help to form habitual heartfelt dispositions to act.
1. Human dignity - our humanity is the basis of our equal dignity. Even someone who has done the wrong thing, or who is being punished, should not be insulted, humiliated, or written off.		
2. Solidarity - we have duty to assist fellow human beings in need. First those closest to us, and whom we can practically help.		
3. Subsidiarity – all have the right to exercise responsibility for their own affairs to the extent they are able; this is a consequence of human dignity. Government should not create a nanny state, but rather assist individuals.		
4. Common good – what is truly good for the individual is good for the state. If my actions harm others, they harm me as well.		
5. Participation – we all have the right to have our opinion taken into account in matters that affect us.		

[P for C: 128

At the Neural Level: Justice

Learning from others

'It is easy to know when someone is impulsive or timid, but when they are self-centred it is much harder to spot.'
Joseph Pieper

At the neural level, justice is supported by systems of empathy, and by cortical areas that support consideration of moral consequences of our actions, and moral decision making. Memory of past experience as well as the reward circuitry triggered by the joy of serving others are implicated. Attentional systems have been conditioned to preferentially attend to the welfare of others.

1. What are the opportunities to develop empathy with others and compassion that daily present themselves to us?

2. What are the opportunities to develop empathy with others and compassion that can be developed in the home?

3. Develop a range of strategies to help a young person foresee the consequences on others of their actions.

4. What are some daily opportunities to give example of joy in serving others.

5. What are practical ways to correct children without taking joy from the family?

Chapter 10

Chapter 10

SOUND JUDGEMENT

'The ideals which have always shone before me and filled me with joy are goodness, beauty and truth.'
Albert Einstein

Discuss with friends

Jimmy had not been a model student to the end of Year 10. He loved surfing and no teacher at school would have backed him to score better than 80th percentile in his end of schooling exams. Yet when his dad walked into his bedroom at the start of Year 11 and saw a large '99' written on paper over his son's desk, he said to his boy, 'I don't want you to be disappointed. Do you think 99 is realistic?'

'Dad, I need a goal.'

In the subsequent two years he was a changed young man, incredibly diligent in his studies. He sat his end of schooling public exams and earned a 98.4 result. It was *his* goal.

Sound judgement, sometimes called prudence or practical reason, is the capacity to set wise, feasible goals for ourselves. There are two aspects to this virtue. On the one hand it is the habit of accepting physical and moral reality, and on the more practical side, it is the habit of making sound judgements about what we will do. The first refers to depth of sincerity, and the second to effective goal setting.

How easy it is to talk ourselves out of duty: 'What a man wishes to believe, he believes to be true' was just as true in the times of Demosthenes as it is now. We create our own realities if we are not sincere. Conscience, and even physical and biological reality, can be denied.

We must never break the connection between truth and love. Cicero wrote about this: 'Knowledge divorced from justice may be called cunning but not wisdom'. How often we prioritise self-serving actions but refuse to admit we are selfish. We can give ourselves reasons for anything.

This is the task of prudence and justice working in concert. Prudence as the *conviction* and justice as a love that moves us to act for what we know to be good and true.
Discuss with friends.

1. Prudence is to capacity to accept in physical and moral reality and being able to set goals for ourselves. What are the biggest challenges faced by parents who wish to teach habits to their children in each of these categories?

2. Fostering prudence requires trusting conversations. How can parents best schedule weekly 1:1 conversations with each child?

[P for C: 53]

Practically Speaking

Prioritise

'The greatest way to live with honour in this world is to be what we appear to be.'
Socrates

This table sets out some of the most obvious areas for growth associated with prudence.

Talk together about how your son or daughter demonstrates with actions the qualities of prudence listed on the left. Tick the relevant boxes. For each of the 'Priority areas', write down in the 'Let's be specific' box a very specific moment you can take advantage of, or action you can take, to help your child develop the relevant habit.

Qualities of Prudence	Current level of development					Priority areas	Let's be specific
	No evidence	Poor	Fair	Quite good	Well developed		
Thinks before acting							
Well-formed conscience							
Finds out the facts before deciding							
Sets own goals							
Rational not emotional							
Knows how to prioritise							
Consults feelings but not led by feelings							
Thinks logically							
Thinks critically about what is read or viewed							
Looks for advice when appropriate							
Wise							
Open minded, and able to listen, respect, and evaluate other opinions							
Has deeply held ideals							

Is flexible about opinionable matters							
Has strongly held convictions about matters that are objectively important							
Sincere with self							
Grounded in reality							
Decisive. Practical in devising practical plans of action							
Reflective and able think critically							
Naturally confident and optimistic							
Flexible							
Loves learning							
Discerning. Able to recognise truth from falsehood							
Mindful. Able to reflect on one's own feelings, dispositions and situation							
Has deeply held convictions based on trust							
Creative							
Deep commitment to truth							
Independently minded							

[P for C: 95]

The Dimensions of Prudence

Brainstorm

Brainstorm some priorities for your parenting focus if you are to raise a child with the full spectrum of good habits associated with the cardinal virtue of prudence.

Virtues within Prudence	Relevant points of focus in your home.
Ability to seek truth and desire to live in reality	
A well-developed conscience and ability to discern good from bad	
Ability to set personal goals	
Sincerity	
Flexibility and readiness to consider the opinions of others	
Readiness to seek advice	
Capacity to reflect	
Idealism	
Mindfulness of own feelings- a detachment that gives objectivity	
Humility	
Optimism and positivity	
Confidence	
Trustworthiness	
Wisdom	

[P for C: 53]

Do I Teach Clearly What is Right and What is Wrong?

Take the test — Brainstorm

> *'Don't just do things with your son, talk to him.'*
> **Martin Fitzgerald**

There are two pathways to good actions: desires and reasons. The first is by way of virtuous desires, where love for what is good, true and beautiful draws us to good actions, and the second is by giving ourselves reasons to act in certain ways. The first is more automatic and can be nurtured by diligent parenting from the earliest years, carefully guiding the dispositions and desires for truth and beauty that are maturing in a child's soul. Crucial in this second pathway is a well-formed conscience. Here we look at formation of conscience.

Can I tick these 10 boxes?

- ☐ Do we give our children a clear understanding of what is right and why? Do we help them distinguish truth and objective reality from opinion and sentiment?
- ☐ Are we conscious of the reasons we give ourselves for acting? Do I learn to look critically at these reasons because we are capable of justifying anything to ourselves?
- ☐ Do we teach our children to value the voice of their conscience, to form it well, and to ask advice from the right persons?
- ☐ Do we grasp the link between humility and truth: a person who 'knows everything' is not open to the truth?
- ☐ Do we give our children guided practice in making choices and decisions? Do I let children make up their own minds unless it is a matter of moral or physical danger? Then do I debrief afterwards, especially if bad choices or mistakes have been made? Do I help my child understand the foolishness and sadness that follows when we deliberately go against what we know in our conscience to be right? Do I explain that deliberate choices to do the wrong thing are very different from impulsive behaviours and are seriously vice forming?
- ☐ Do we provide positive cyber education where children are protected but also where they build up the wherewithal to take control of their situation?
- ☐ Do I offer careful ongoing guidance based on trusting dialogue between us? Do I gently encourage my child to open his or her heart, to talk about what they are thinking and experiencing? This is the prerequisite for all effective education.
- ☐ Am I sincerity with myself about situations that lead me to drop my guard, offending God and others - for example in times of tiredness, or self-pity? Do I recognise these situations and take steps to avoid them or remove myself? Do we teach these skills to our children?
- ☐ Do we honour our commitments? Do I carry out my duties and jobs? Do I give and keep my promises aware that promises are publicly witnessed goals that will help me achieve good things in our lives?
- ☐ Do we teach our children the importance of honouring a promise, a commitment, or a contract, and the power that it brings with it to do good things for others?

[P for C: 84]

Take Conversation Seriously with a Small Child

Parent-child talk

'My father was accustomed to shape me as a boy by words.'
Horace

Do you take conversation with a small child seriously? Don't just *do* things with your son or daughter: *create times you talk easily*. Do you have *ongoing* conversations? Do you try to foresee the big issues that will be arising in only a few years, and give clear age-appropriate guidelines preparing the ground for more complete discussions later about challenges your child will face: faith, drugs, internet, attitudes to sexuality and relationships, business ethics, modesty, etc.

Reinforce life lessons:

- Be kind to all.
- Don't get sloppy with the details... it is proof that you care.
- People are more important than things.
- Doing good things makes us happy.
- We value the people and things when we pay attention to them.
- Love is to give of oneself. Life is about loving and giving.
- Work is service.
- Family is a place where we always help each other.

Over a cup of coffee with your spouse, if you can, list a variety of different ways to reinforce these life lessons. What other life lessons would you add to this list?

1. _____

2. _____

3. _____

[P for C: 16]

Conversation with a Seven-Year-Old

'By the efforts parents make to connect when a child is younger, they earn the right to be part of their teenager's life.'
Bruce Robinson, *Fathering in the Fast Lane*

Rank yourself 0 (worst) to 5 (outstanding) for the following 20 questions.

____ Do you talk 1:1 daily, and give dedicated time for a longer chat weekly?

____ Do you work at getting to know your son or daughter? Favourite colour? Favourite animal? What do they want to be when they grow up? What makes them happy? Their favourite thing? Their favourite place? Where they would go if they could go anywhere? Who they would be if they could be anyone? If they ran the world, the rules they would have? What makes them sad? What makes them angry? Do you know the name of your son's or daughter's best friend? And then ask another question about the answer.

____ Are you a good listener and take conversation seriously with a seven-year-old?

____ Do you make eye contact and talk about their world?

____ Do you know how to talk enthusiastically and light up the conversation?

____ Do you know when to use 'how' and 'why' questions?

____ Are you aware of the skills you need to communicate even better?

____ Do you try not to go on car trips alone...not even to the shops? Do you use regular trips to talk, to sport practice, to the shops, or to school?

____ Do you share activities you both like?

____ Do you avoid correcting in front of younger brothers and sisters?

____ Do you talk to your son or daughter as you want them to be, not as they are now?

____ Do you give real reasons? Your child will need to give himself or herself reasons.

____ Do you talk clearly about what is right and what is wrong?

____ Have you learned to tell a good story? Do you tell moral stories very often?

____ Do you talk passionately ideals, the nobility of great people and great qualities of character?

____ Do you talk enthusiastically of beauty and art?

____ Do you teach your child what it means to be beautiful on the inside?

____ Do you speak with humility?

____ Do you talk glowingly of other family members always?

Total_____

If your total is >80 things are probably on track.

If not take the quiz again in 6 months to see if you have improved.

[P for C: 16]

Talking with a Ten-Year-Old

'It is the duty of parents to emotionally nourish their children. It is not the role of children to emotionally nourish their parents.'
Ross Campbell

Are you moving with the times? Has your communication adapted?

____ Do you talk 1:1 daily, and give dedicated time for a longer chat weekly?

____ Do you give real reasons as your child will need to give himself or herself reasons to act?

____ Do you talk enthusiastically about what you have discovered that is good, true and beautiful?

____ Do you talk about inspiring people and deeds?

____ Do you consult their opinion very often?

____ Do you put your spouse on a pedestal in all conversation?

____ Do you help them set goals for themselves each week?

____ Do you know how to ask open ended questions that launch them into conversation?

____ Do you know what the joys and challenges of today have been for your son or daughter?

____ Do you make a point of broadening your child's interests by sharing your interests not by being a know-all?

____ Do you use informal chats to pass on charitable ways of looking at people, concern to help others, the need for determination and will power, sincerity, and cheerfulness… remembering that, while your example is the best teacher, what you say does have an impact?

____ Do you take advantage of car trips to open your heart about things important to you and your spouse?

____ Do you develop an interest in their hobbies and their sports?

____ Do you talk about the things you do together because your child's interests are your interests? Do you work on combined projects?

____ Do we have enthusiastic conversation about the things we have both read because there is a culture of reading at home, and we often go to the library.

____ Are you good at showing affection? Or do you show affection in the problematic ways… babying spoiling, excusing selfish behaviour, over-cuddling and smothering a child who needs to learn independence?

____ Do you guide your child to do things independently? Do you forget that the more we love a child, often it means doing less for them, not more.

____ Do you pick your battles, holding calmly and with good humour to reasonable expectations: doing one's job, helping in the kitchen, sorting out one's things, looking after one's belongings, keeping focused on a simple goal, etc.

____ Do we remind ourselves that a parent's moodiness, tendency to impatience or anger can have a serious effect on the confidence that becoming-adolescent will show? A parent who is dogmatic, who prefers to talk rather than listen, who talks about himself or herself too much, or is too easily critical of the efforts, interests and friends of the child will start to find that child progressively more reluctant to communicate.

____ Have you made sure that your child has learned the facts of life from you or your spouse by the time he or she is ten years old? By 12 they will need a clear understanding of the mistakes into which people can fall.

Total_____

If your total is >80 things are probably on track.

If not take the quiz again in 6 months to see if you have improved.

[P for C: 93]

Why is My Child Not Truthful?

Reflect

Heart to Heart

'The end of an ox is beef, and the end of a lie is grief.'
African quotation

Sincerity is essential if we are to seek and recognise the truth about ourselves, and if we are to form permanent relationships with others. Sincerity underpins the virtue of prudence allowing a young person to think for themselves. It is essential in relationships, helping us see our deficiencies, recognise and admit faults and make apologies, and set appropriate goals for future action. When we are unable to face truth we deceive ourselves and others. We will be frustrated in our very nature because we have an intellect that seeks truth but has lost the will to seek truth, and act on it. Confucius described sincerity as 'the basis of every virtue'. For the same reason, the Romans called prudence the chariot driver of the four horses of virtue: reality must guide our self-knowledge and every choice we make.

Audit your own example.

- Am I honest, no ifs no buts?
- Am I honest with myself or do I sometimes say one thing but do another?
- Do I live in reality, or a reality of my own making?
- Do I ever lie to avoid trouble?
- Do I accept excuses from myself, or from our children?
- I must consider where my child could be learning to behave in a way that is not sincere. Is this child scared of the consequences? Scared of me? Does the child have a habit of copying the insincerity of others, of older children, of children at school? Has there been a pattern of small insincerities that I have been missing?

5-7 years old

Many parents find that at this age their child has a 'natural' honesty, but that this can regress if bad habits are learned! Often it is best not to confront a child of this age with choice of telling you a lie or not. Try not to back them into a corner. Rather let the child know that you know they did something they should not have and you will not allow that misbehaviour. (But do be sure of your facts.)

In these years don't let habits of not telling the truth develop. Some mums notice that many children seem to go through a stage around these years or a little earlier where they lie. We should understand this but insist on the truth. Remind your child that you were six or seven once... you know a story when you hear one. Make eye contact - it makes it more difficult for a child to lie. Be sensitive to the *possibility* that your son's suspected lying is really a product of forgetfulness or dreaming.

- When talking, make eye contact - it makes it more difficult for a child to lie.
- Teach that saying sorry is the best way to fix things up.
- Teach that we must love the truth, and never fear being honest.
- Ensure there is reward as well as punishment. Show that honesty will be treated with love and respect.

- Don't harp back to earlier mistakes.
- To help children never be afraid of telling the truth because of the punishment, ask 'What do you think is a fair punishment?'
- Explain the consequences of telling lies.
- Forgiveness – don't punish for telling the truth about a wrongdoing and give praise for courage of telling the truth/give child a way out.

7-8 years old.

By the time a child is seven or eight they should not be telling untruths. They are old enough to know better. Address this energetically. The clock is ticking. If a child of this age still is not truthful or has significant slip-ups, reflect on the reasons.

- Do you have all the important facts? Is the child being truthful from his or her perspective?
- Are your high expectations supported by affection? Stay calm and reassuring but don't accept 'I forgot', or vague evasions.
- When you caught the child out being insincere did you talk calmly, explain your disappointment and quickly give them an opportunity to redeem your trust? Did you help a child learn to put things right with a personal apology.
- Is the child fearful of your reaction, or of getting into trouble? Do they have a memory of getting you very upset about something else?
- Hate the sin; love the sinner. Distinguish between the fault and the person committing the fault: persons are always shown patience and kindness.
- If emotions are running high, allow time for them to dissipate. It can help too to continue the conversation in a different place.
- Is the child's behaviour an exaggeration of your own behaviour? For example do you avoid having two faces: one for the family and one for business.
- Is this a behaviour learned from peers or siblings? Remember, children will imitate anyone who spends time with them, even virtually.
- Do you know how to help your child look at the causes and consequences, to others especially, of his or her actions?

[P for C: 24]

Giving Small Children Choices

'Virtue is the perfection of reason.'
St Augustine

Resist the temptation to over-manage children. Children who are denied frequent practice in decision making will be under-prepared for life. Don't do the thinking for them. Younger children who don't have practice thinking for themselves won't be able to make good decisions as teenagers, and by then the stakes are much higher.

Can you tick these 15 boxes?

- ☐ Am I deeply interested in what my child has to say?
- ☐ Do I have the patience to have serious conversation with a small child? Am I convinced that every word, spoken at the right time, is going in?
- ☐ Do I know how to create these times?
- ☐ Do I give choices to a young child? Try this pattern for a few weeks:
  1. Give simple directions, an A or B choice, when the child is in front of you.
  2. Speak face to face.
  3. Make eye contact.
  4. Request to do it now.
  5. Verify.
- ☐ By listening to my child's interests and observations do we end up having deep conversations?
- ☐ Do I teach my child to check their feelings against facts and reality?
- ☐ Am I convinced that no one else has the right to set the moral education agenda for my child?
- ☐ Do I understand that the habit of critical reasoning requires also a commitment to discriminate between truth and falsehood, between right and wrong?
- ☐ Do I consult my child's opinions, even if eventually we decide something differently?
- ☐ Do I manipulate? Am I more interested in getting the result that I want than in forming the heart and mind of my child?
- ☐ Do I give honest and real reasons, or do I just shoot from the hip?
- ☐ Do I give good reasons or fall into the mistake of saying, 'Do it because I said so'?
- ☐ Do I form my child's capacity for critical thinking and depth of understanding by talking about things they notice around them - billboards, books, television programs and news?
- ☐ Do I help my child have simple goals in their use of time?
- ☐ Do I sow a love for service and generosity in my child?

[P for C: 78]

Teach Humility

Heart to Heart

Prioritise

'The unexamined life is not worth living.'
Socrates

Humility is essential if we are to seek and recognise the truth about ourselves. It starts with recognising that I am a creature who has been given so much, and so I have the duty to honour and thank my creator Father. And from this also flows the truth about myself... that I am loved, and we are children of God. All our strength 'is on loan'.

We teach humility by thinking more about others than about ourselves, by giving importance to others and by being a gracious host and generous friend, by our readiness to apologise first, by thinking little of the inconvenience to ourselves when we see a need. In practice in our home we can focus on:

_____

We teach humility by our own self-restraint, by not overplaying our hand, by not wanting to be the centre of attention, by a natural reluctance to talk about ourselves in a good light, by making light of difficulties or slights, by avoiding adult tantrums of impatience or crankiness. In practice in our home we can focus on:

_____

We teach humility when we seek the truth, when we avoid moulding reality according to our preferences, when we acknowledge a Creator and so an objective ground to truth and goodness, and beauty. In practice in our home we can focus on:

_____

We teach humility when we give a child the example of striving constantly to be a better person. It is more important to show children how to overcome weaknesses, than to appear unrealistically perfect. For dad that may means asking his wife's suggestions, striving to be home for family dinner most nights of the week, putting initiative into family life each weekend, mowing the lawns before being reminded, and following up the responsibilities delegated to children. For mum it may mean inviting feedback, putting initiative into family life each weekend. In practice in our home we can focus on:

Dad	Mum
1. _____	1. _____
2. _____	2. _____
3. _____	3. _____

[P for C: xii]

Humble and Confident

Case studies

Invite some friends for supper and use these case studies as discussion starters.

> Mildred, in Year 6, is somewhat of a busybody. She tends to offer opinions when not asked and has a nasty way of hurting others with her words. In fact in the past term, her classmates have started to exclude her from games. They avoid working with her in groups in the class even though she is clever. Mildred claims she is being bullied and her father is quick to say as much to his friends.

1. How can a teacher address these issues and also work with the father of Max?

2. What character strengths seem to be needed for Max, and for his classmates?

> Lief is a new boy in Year 6. Perhaps because he is new, you notice that he does not seem totally at ease with his peers when you have boys in the class over after school. He is polite and well-presented and seems conscientious about his work when you talk to him. At the school fête you exchange impressions with the parents, who arrived in Australia the year before. It seems that in Year 5 Lief had a difficult time in another school and for that reason they moved him. You are surprised but a little saddened to learn that Lief is very nervous about coming to school each morning. He will not catch the bus, and he is totally embarrassed by his shiny black shoes (polished by his mother every night) that he puts them in his bag, and wears runners to walk from his front door to the car in case any students from his previous school should see him.

1. How could you constructively progress this conversation?

2. What qualities of character would potentially assist Lief and how could they be developed?

[P for C: 141]

Subtle Pressures

Family activity — Family Meeting

'Where so many hours have been spent in convincing myself that I am right, is there not some reason to fear I may be wrong?'
Jane Austen, *Sense and Sensibility*

In what ways are we being subtly manipulated by the media, and by public role models, to think certain things? To feel certain emotions? To act in particular ways?

Here are some ways to help young people become aware of the subtle manipulation they are being subjected to:

- When you are in the car, play 'I spy' with a difference: Spot bus shelter ads that manipulate our feelings and emotions and explain the emotion that is being targeted.
- Play a game at dinner time. When you ask for something you must precede the request by evoking an emotion: 'How happy it will make you to pass me the salt!' 'How good you make me feel if you pass me the milk.' 'How powerful you look when you do the washing up. Will you do that?' 'How incredible you will be if you can bring both the brush and the pan.' Don't repeat the emotion word that someone else has used.

Can you think of other strategies you can bring into your family?

[P for C: 16]

Core Thinking Skills Can be Learned

Parent-child talk

'Knowledge becomes evil if the aim be not virtuous.'
Plato

Practise these skills with your child. Children who have been taught to think are much better at problem solving and at seeing all the possible options. Try to think of another local example you can refer to.

- Remember that most disagreements occurred because of sloppy definitions.
    - When someone talks about human rights see if they are talking about 'the rights we all have from our common humanity', or if they are misusing the term; for example, it is a human right to receive treatment for pain, but it not a human right to kill oneself. I have a right to protect myself, but not a right to carry an assault rifle. I have a right to family life but that right brings responsibilities to others. I have a right to sufficient food to live, but not a right to indulge myself. Rights can be abused very easily

- Teach children to separate facts from opinion.
    - Talk about the headline articles.
    - Ask 'Is that fact or opinion?'

- Teach disciplined habits of approaching problems.
    - Show how planning a holiday can be broken down into parts.

- Teach how to brainstorm for options and to rationally select the option with the most advantages.
    - Demonstrate the worth of listing pros and cons for different possibilities.

- Show how to put down plans, goals, and options on paper, so as to be better able to assess them and remember them. Help your child to appreciate the priceless treasure of order: on one's desk, but more importantly in one's mind.
    - Show that writing things enables us to organize our thoughts.

- Peace in our hearts comes from order in our lives. The fundamental order is that our actions, our feelings, and our convictions are all in step.
    - Help a young person be mindful of feelings and emotions generated by advertisements that seek to manipulate us.

[P for C: 128]

Sorting Out the Real From the Woke

Parent-child talk

'A wise man makes his own decisions. An ignorant man follows public opinion.'
Chinese proverb

How many arguments and mistakes can be avoided if we think clearly. Gradually teach these skills. Think up examples in the life of your child that you can use to illustrate the points below in conversations with your child.

Coach a child to distinguish the *reality* of a situation from opinions and feelings.

- Teach children to recognise facts. This helps them to avoid decisions based on incomplete information, emotion or personal prejudice. Play observation, concentration and memory games. When you need to know 'What happened?' insist on main facts not trivia. Ask not only 'What do you know about this?' but also 'How do you know?'
- Teach that it is quite possible to be passionate about something and completely wrong.
- Show that emotions are a marvellous help to engage with others. They can give us great determination to act, but they are not reliable guides for the truth.
- Some things are absolutes, others are opinionable where there is a prudential path to be followed. Be very clear about the difference.
- We need to learn to make our own decisions in opinionable matters because prudent action is best discerned by the person directly involved. Give children practice in making these choices. Then help them evaluate the results.
- Teach the difference between aims and objectives. Teach how to put down plans, goals and options on paper, so as to be better able to assess them and remember them.
- Teach Edward De Bono's coloured hats as a way of opening up issues. De Bono argues that children who have been taught to think are much better at problem solving and at seeing all the possible options.
- Teach how to brainstorm for options and to rationally select the option with the most advantages. Teach mind mapping.
- Teach children to separate facts from opinion, between objectivity and subjectivity, between feelings and reasons, between emotion and rationality.
- Teach about the difference between data, hypotheses, and facts.
- Teach that in the natural world, there are three ways we normally know reality: by our senses, by reasoning, and by trust in the word of persons we know to be trustworthy. We assess trustworthiness either because our experience with that person confirms their credibility or because of recommendations from others we already trust.
- Think before you speak.
- Demonstrate that most disagreements occur because of sloppy definitions.
- Don't exaggerate issues, over dramatise or emotionalise problems, or 'catastrophise'.
- Teach disciplined habits of approaching problems. Teach the micro skills of problem solving: Walk your child through the process of breaking a problem up into parts, of consulting stakeholders, of brainstorming, of forming a plan, of evaluating progress on the plan, of revising the strategy.
- Teach that self-knowledge, reflection and decision precede personal change, and that our desires are only as good as our concrete plans and readiness to implement intermediate steps.

[P for C: 147]

Maxims for Life

Discuss with friends

Some families have Maxims like: 'Do what you do, do well', 'What is honourable is difficult', 'Serve others first', or 'There is more happiness in giving than taking'

What are Maxims in your family, sayings that you encourage your children to live by. And how are you teaching each of these sayings?

An example is completed for you:

Maxim	Five strategies to teach this:
'Carry your weather with you'	Dad tries to model cheerfulness on arriving back from work.
	Remind your child to call out bad behaviour, but to find excuses for people caught up in it.
	Talk at afternoon tea about what happened at school each day.
	Remind how doing things for others makes us happy.
	Mum models cheerfulness at peak hour before dinner.

[P for C: 138]

At the Neural Level: Prudence

Learning from others

'Overall, research is confirming that exceptional performers are not necessarily endowed with superior brains. Rather, the brain–thanks to its plasticity–can be modified by deliberate practice.'
Dr Robert Restak

At the neural level, prudence is mediated by neurobiological processes, systems and pathways for holding convictions in memory, for goal election and for deliberation of means to realise these goals, supported by the systems and pathways associated with the virtues of temperance, fortitude, and justice.

1. In what ways can adults fall into the trap of living in a make-believe world?

2. What are very specific and practical ways to teach a young child to distinguish right from wrong?

3. What are very specific and practical ways to teach ten- to twelve-year-old to distinguish right from wrong?

4. What are reasonable areas where a five-year-old can set goals for himself or herself?

5. What are reasonable areas where a ten-year-old should be setting goals for himself or herself?

Chapter 11

SELF-GIVING: THE TASK OF ADOLESENCE

'Self-knowledge leads to self-mastery which leads to self-giving.'
David Isaacs

Discuss with friends

Teenage years are tough... spur-of-the-moment actions easily trump sensible choice, sometimes with catastrophic results. One young policeman speaks of the incident that brought him to resign. He and a fellow constable were on duty, walking through a shopping centre, in a tougher area of Sydney.

'A young guy, maybe 13 or 14 years old, is in front of us. Suddenly he has a gun in his hand pointing at my buddy. Of course I react. I draw my pistol. I am about to fire, and the kid waves this gun and says, "It's only a replica. It's only a replica." A half second more and he would have been dead. It was a nightmare.'

Teenagers are prone to do things they regret. We have all been there. Virtues take time to develop. We need practice consolidating pathways of emotional restraint. We need the guidance of good mentoring. And we also need experience to know that certain actions may lead to consequences completely out of our control. A naïve young person late alone late on Friday night public transport may get more than they bargained for.

We have a much better chance however of stepping around the bear pits and making good decisions if we are masters of ourselves. Plutarch, a Greek writing in Roman times, has given us perhaps the best definition of adolescence: 'For intelligent people the passage from childhood to adulthood is not an abandonment of rules, but a change of ruler'. The former Roman slave Epictetus, captured this same idea in his aphorism, 'No man is free who is not master of himself'. The key task of parenting teens is to foster this self-rule, and so, less beholden to external pressures, less inhibited by irrational fears, but also less distracted by our untrained passions.

Freedom is not an end itself. It is only when we are self-directing that can we love by choice, not by impulse.

Discuss with friends.

1. Why is self-mastery so difficult for so many teenagers? Pick the biggest challenges and offer several ways that parents can help.

2. How can we help teens experience the joy that comes from generosity and serving others? Much depends on this.

[P for C: 109]

What's Different Now?

Reflect

'The young person has three main characteristics: he is idealistic, a person of extremes and exaggerated attitudes, and he is attracted to what is new.'
Aristotle

less to more obvious in our child					Features of adolescence
					self-absorption, moodiness, introspection, indifference to others
					insecurity...peer dependence, impressionability, wanting to be noticed, comparisons with others
					anxiety and confusion...feelings of being unhappy, emotional and temperamental
					lack of motivation, laziness, possible less engagement with schooling
					need for affection and attention, forming superficial relationships
					yearning for greater independence,
					argumentative, contesting authority, pulling back from parents
					idealism
					discovery of autonomy, initiative and goal setting
					investment in personal relationships outside the family
					a growing awareness of self and one's own opinions, and values
					development of a capacity for critical thinking
					noticeably adopting values for adult life
					sexual awakening
					increasing exposure to technological media
					challenges with impulse control and delaying gratification
					a reduced capacity to maintain focussed attention
					easily swayed by sentiment and emotion
					more aware of material and consumer attractions
					self-conscious

[P for C: 110]

Be Positive

'Fathers, do not drive your children to resentment'
Eph 6:4

Adolescence should be the most marvellous time for self-awakening. Consider what can get in the way of this? How are you tracking in your family?

The great self-awakening of adolescence	The great traps for parents	Goals for your own parenting
The discovery of self, the personal world that is proper to human existence.... *'I am a person, with my own mind, my own heart, my own personality'*.	Do not focus on the superficial changes of adolescence (appearance, self absorption, anxiety, lack of motivation, etc) while being ignorant of the great interior drama being played out - just when a young person needs guidance and affection in a challenging time.	
The discovery of freedom and the responsibilities that this brings... *'I am autonomous, free to take my life in the direction I want'*. But the outcome, a free and capable human being, is marvellous.	Instead of guiding their teen, parents can mistakenly respond to a young person's natural yearning for freedom either by permissive absence of guidance, or by clamping down without an appreciation of the need to respect their child's growing autonomy and responsibility.	
The discovery of the values a young person chooses that will take him or her through life.	Just when teenagers are in need of a strong connection with their parents and with the values in which they were raised, parent-child trust and communication can be at their worst. If parents themselves are distracted by work or their difficulties in their own relationships, the outcome can be very ugly.	

[P for C: 126]

Let's be Specific

Prioritise

Heart to Heart

> 'Teens have the power to determine their own brain development, to determine which connections survive and which don't (by) whether they do art, or music, or sports, or video games.'
> **JM Schwartz and S Begley, *The Mind and the Brain***

Talk together about the parental qualities that help teenagers. Tick the relevant boxes. For each of the 'Priority areas' that you identify, drill down to very specific moments you can take advantage of, or action you can take, to help your child develop the relevant habit.

A CHECKLIST FOR RAISING TEENAGERS WITH CHARACTER	Level of Development in your family					Priority areas
	Well developed	Fair to middling	Fair	Much work needed	Non-existing	
We have a positive view of adolescence. We don't focus our attention on the superficial features.						
We address the immediate needs of our child.						
We are focused on the long-term need to build strong habits and convictions.						
We are striving to prepare even younger children for the challenge of thinking for themselves and running their own lives.						
We are convinced of our teenage child's potential to do great things for others. This confidence is tangible.						
We own up to our innermost values.						
We strive to live out the happiness that our values should deliver.						
We realise that teenagers change on the inside first.						
We keep the focus on having our teenagers think, rather than obliging his or her conformity to our wishes.						
We help our son or daughter internalise the process of developing good habits.						
We are creative in our ways to keep communicating effectively.						
We address issues without putting off difficult conversations.						

We explain reasons.						
We strive to lay foundations for a positive peer group around our son or daughter.						
We do our best to work in close partnership with our child's school.						
We seek out mentors who have the confidence of our son or daughter.						
We keep our focus on building resilient habits of hardiness, problem solving and self-control.						
We give our son or daughter a first-class ongoing preparation for relationships and sexuality						
We live up to our duty to provide unconditional daily affection.						
We model peace in the face of life's greatest challenges						

[P for C: 112]

When Your Child is Becoming a Teenager

Learning from others

'The I-You relation is both distinctive of persons and also constitutive of them.'
Roger Scruton

Am I sincere with myself about the values that dominate my life... am I striving to give of myself at every level: in my faith, living for my wife and family, seeing my job as service to others, sharing my things, being ready to defer the things I enjoy for the sake of others? Lived values, more than specific behaviours, will be passed on.

1. Do I show that my values bring genuine and manifest happiness?
2. Do I know how to give my adolescent child affection?
3. Does my child feel deeply appreciated? And do I appreciate the great changes taking place on the inside or am I just focused on what I see and hear?
4. Do I put more emphasis on guiding my teenage child to think for himself or herself rather than simply conform? Do I explain reasons?
5. How do I teach the lifelong importance of pushing oneself to develop good habits?
6. Do I invest all the time that is needed to become a close friend of my son or daughter?
7. Do I address issues or just hope that everything works out well? Do I talk deeply. The clock is ticking.
8. Do we speak trustingly in depth about human love, about purity of heart, and of love as the sincere gift of oneself?
9. Do I sincerely pray about my son or daughter often, and for them, every day?

These questions are inspired by Prof David Isaacs, the author of *Character Building*.

[P for C: 114]

Fostering Motivation

Case study

'Nothing moves us to love as much as the awareness of being loved.'
St Thomas Aquinas

Invite some friends for supper and use this case study as a discussion starter.

> Beatrix is a delightful but disorganised, or perhaps lazy, girl... her teachers are not sure which. When the Year 11 parent teacher night arrives, Elspeth, her geography teacher, talks frankly to her mother, 'I cannot get any essays from Beatrix.' She receives a helpless response, 'I can't do anything. She just lies on her bed every afternoon flicking through Instagram.' The next day Elspeth decides to take matters into her own hands. 'Beatrix, we need to talk about the five essays you owe me.' 'O Miss, I want to do the work but I lack self-motivation.'

1. Help Elspeth help Beatrix. What can she suggest or do?

2. When Elspeth meets Beatrix's mother at the shop the next week, the mother asks for suggestions to help her daughter. What can Elspeth say?

[P for C: 143]

The Risk Matrix of Adolescent Bearpits

Prioritise

Heart to Heart

Michael, the father of one of my former students, was working in the field of risk mitigation. On reading in the news story of a girl who answered an ad that had been posted by her future killer, he voiced a scalding assessment of her parents:

'Her parents had no idea. This is sad for everyone involved but real. I often hear parents complain: "Can't the police do something?" What the parents should ask is what they have done to alert their children in the first place. This girl died because she was plain stupid, but her parents and family even more so. Raising naïve adults is sad. You should not live your children's lives but at least alert them to the reality of life. The stories that I hear of fraud on gullible people make me cringe.'

How can we forearm a child against such tragedies. How can parents create the depth of communication which is such a duty of parenthood?

We must be the decisive influence on each son and daughter. Is this asking too much? Isn't it hard enough just to stay in the game? Remember the aim is to build habits of communication, not one-offs. This is a risk matrix that allows you to classify risks according to their likelihood, and seriousness. It is a convenient way of analysing the challenges.

		Potential Impact				
		Negligible	Marginal	Serious	Critical	Catastrophic
Likelihood	Certain					
	Highly Probable					
	Likely					
	Unlikely					
	Most unlikely					

Here are the top Parental Health Concerns according to Mott Polling in 2017. Discuss with your spouse whether any constitute real risks for your own teen and place the number in the appropriate square in the Matrix. Risks falling in the shaded zones are potentially the most serious.

1. Bullying/cyberbullying (61%)
2. Not enough exercise (60%)
3. Unhealthy eating (57%)
4. Drug abuse (56%)
5. Internet safety (55%)
6. Child abuse and neglect (53%)
7. Suicide (45%)
8. Depression (44%)
9. Teen pregnancy (43%)

10. Anxiety and stress (43%)

Here are some garden-variety challenges although consequences can be disproportionately nasty. Which of these do you regard as significant risks for your son or daughter? Position them also in the matrix.

11. Acting without thinking. Brain explosions... dumb choices. Lack of thought of consequences of actions. Lack of self-control.
12. Avoidance of difficult things.
13. Selfishness. Self-centredness. Habits of unkindness to others.
14. Insincerity. Being closed off to parents.
15. Discourtesy to family members. Lack of interpersonal consideration.
16. A succession of bad school reports.
17. Not setting goals for oneself.
18. Lack of perseverance in work.
19. Fads, ads and commercialism.
20. Insecurity and peer-attention-seeking actions.
21. Passivity... laziness, television, games and late assignments.
22. Pornography. Lack of deep respect for the great gift of sexuality.
23. Temper
24. Self-harm
25. Lack of confidence
26. Negativity
27. Confusion about gender
28. Confusion about religious belief and parental values
29. Boredom... losing interest in activities once enjoyable
30. Fatigue
31. Irritability
32. Loss of appetite
33. Loss or gaining of weight
34. Low self-esteem: feelings of worthlessness, guilt, or hopelessness.
35. Persistent low mood

Now study the risks you have placed in shaded zones. What plans can you put in place to mitigate them? Be open to seeking expert advice.

Remember that teenage years are about learning self-management, but parents still have the duty to keep their teen safe from serious (or worse) consequences of actions carried out through inexperience or thoughtlessness, or simply through weakness of character. It is important to say 'no' in cases of physical or moral danger. But be close enough to your child so that they trust your judgement. You can no longer parent by edict!

Shaded zone risk assessments		
Number	**Risk**	**Actions you will take to mitigate the risks**
		•
		•
		•

Now keep yourself accountable.

[P for C: 145]

Communicating with Teenagers

Take the test — Brainstorm

'Young men must be overcome by reason not by force.'
Publius Syrus

Are these statements true in your own family? Go through them as a couple.

- ☐ Teenage boys and girls both need individual time with dad because it is the job of dad to show what a good man is and thinks.
- ☐ *'If the parents' job is to prepare their children for independence, staying too close is bound to undermine the process.'* (Hugh Mackay)
- ☐ Dads often need to work harder than mums to keep open communication with their teenage sons. Many boys can feel more understood by their mums, and believe they understand their mums better.
- ☐ *'The bottom line in our communication is that I want not only to teach self-discipline and teach teenagers to think for themselves, but to raise them to love others.'*
- ☐ Teenage girls feel special if they have 1:1 time with dad.
- ☐ We use our chats also to give ongoing sex education and advice. We feel it is only right for a young person to learn the most intimate truths of human love from his or her parents, and that unnecessary problems will arise if this does not happen.
- ☐ Teenage children can be discouraged by what they see as a parents' moodiness, negativity, tiredness, stress, or impatience. They can interpret these things as obstacles to communication.
- ☐ Everyone needs affection but the expressions of affection vary.
- ☐ *'Communication is best with mum when she is open with me.'*
- ☐ Children treasure moments when we take them into our confidence and speak sincerely and deeply about one's own life, love for one's spouse, faith. Relaxed one to one talk builds trust.
- ☐ *'The best time for communication with dad is when he comes home from work at night, and we have a chat about each other's day.'*
- ☐ Ninety percent of communication must be positive. It is more positive sometimes to look forward rather than backwards. It is rarely productive to harp on what has gone wrong or to refer to past mistakes.
- ☐ *'I only tell my teenager what to do if it is a question of physical or moral danger. I other matters I let them make up their minds, and they know this.'*
- ☐ One to one time with mum and dad is crucial. We all need to feel listened to and under stood. The older a teenager gets, the more it shows if they are not feeling understood at home.
- ☐ Chat needs also be about deeper things. If someone asked 'What is the best thing your parents have ever said to you?' What do you think your teen would say?

[P for C: 104]

Sit on the Same Side of the Table

Parent-child talk

'Knowledge which is acquired under compulsion has no hold on the mind.'
Plato

Helping your teenager in their final years of school.

- Always when it comes to talking about school or school reports, 'sit on the same side of the table' as your teenager. You are not an adversary. You are their biggest fan and supporter (so you have a right also to talk bluntly with boundless affection). Help them respond to information the school gives by helping them set appropriate goals for themselves.
- Help them see the beautiful qualities they are bringing to the world. Help them want to discover the mission to put those qualities at the service of others.
- Don't nag. Occasional deep heart to heart conversations help greatly to guide a young person in his or her choices.
    - Adulthood requires internalised motivation. An adult must learn to act from conviction, reflecting on the choices and freely choosing the best options.
    - The very process of senior school, with its pace of work responsibly undertaken, builds character. Demands bring with them opportunities for character growth. Growth comes through striving, not from staying comfortable.
    - Study should not be for selfish reasons. Without ideals we become selfish and introspective. Students are preparing themselves to serve others: their family and their country.
    - We must not fall into the mistake of thinking that success is proportional to marks. Hard working, unselfish people are much more likely to be happy in life than those who simply pulled in big marks. Students who are responsible in their studies both maximise marks and lay essential foundations of virtue.
    - Beyond a certain age nobody has to keep studying. It would be extremely bad for a young person to spend two years at school without his or her heart in it, entrenching habits of laziness and irresponsibility that would continue well into adulthood. All young persons need to find something into which they throw themselves ... for some it will be school, for others an apprenticeship, or whatever.
    - Do not make excuses for your teenager who is well capable of achieving acceptable application grades in every subject. It is his or her problem... life will throw far greater dilemmas at them, and they need to be ready.
    - Help them reflect on what is happening. Help them to know their own strengths (virtues) and shortcomings (a tendency to be lazy, procrastinate, not face issues, or whatever), and to set their own goals.
- Never, never forget however that school is not life. You are not raising a teenager to do well at school, you are raising them to give of themselves, to love wisely with all their heart and being. All else will follow.

[P for C: 152]

So Much to Talk About

Parent-child talk

'Love is beauty of the soul.'
St Augustine

Tick off these topics as you talk about them with your teenager. Prepare your thoughts beforehand although it is impossible to script a conversation like this. Listen and engage.

- ☐ Truth is objective. Religious faith, through texts such as the Ten Commandments, guides us to get the morality right, but morality is determined by what is objectively good for human nature. Basic moral insights do not depend on time, places, persons, or beliefs. They are universal.
- ☐ Truth is to be defended... always. Never compromise on truth. Talk about your own life experiences in this area.
- ☐ Life is sacred... always. Speak from the heart about the beauty of life, of the tragedy of an anti-life mentality that is destructive and fearful, and that harms the people involved as well as the society as a whole. The end can never justify the means. A doctor's role is to heal and preserve life, never to cause death.
- ☐ Love is gift of self. Giving of oneself in relationships leads to happiness. We either live for others or for ourselves. Love may or may not be associated with feelings, but it is always linked to commitments.
- ☐ We are made for happiness, but happiness is a result, never a goal. It is a result of loving generously. Freedom is a great human good. Only if we are free can we give of ourselves in loving relationships.
- ☐ Talk about the great privilege to know that there is someone else in this world who loves you and gives themselves entirely for you. Cheating is so wrong. Pornography and self-indulgent sex are the diametric opposite of loving relationships. Prepare the reasons and speak from the heart.
- ☐ Talk about mental health. Talk about ways to talk to and help a friend with depression. Talk about the signs. Understand when clinical intervention is needed.
- ☐ Discuss what it means to put Christian values and ethical principles into the world and the workplace. Talk about how some laws can be bad laws and give examples. Discuss ways to have one's say.
- ☐ Love unites, hatred divides. This is true for families and for trouble spots in the world. Living in harmony requires, apologies, forgiveness, and the effort to dialogue and to understand others.
- ☐ Apart from protecting ourselves from violence, it is never right to use violence to solve a problem.
- ☐ Happiness is not in things. Beyond a certain level of income happiness does not increase. What detachment means in practice.
- ☐ Freedom and happiness. Freedom means making choices and sticking to them. Moderation and its antithesis: allowing ourselves to fall into addictions, and compulsive habits. Temperance leaves us 'free to love'. Forewarn against baggage from behaviours that we are too weak to resist because of habits and external pressures.
- ☐ Respect is due to all human beings regardless of their actions. Why torture is wrong. Why 'writing people off' is wrong. The purpose of punishment must be 'medicinal', to help the

person, and restore justice.
- ☐ Work is service, so work comes before play. Work is a great privilege.

- ☐ As creatures we owe eternal gratitude to our maker. Speak from the heart about how God looks after us as a father, provides for us the means to live in a loving relationship with him.
- ☐ We must strive to rule our lives by our head not our feelings. Piety takes effort...and we cannot allow feelings to stop us praying. Building up habits of prayer and sacraments.
- ☐ Understanding suffering.. Suffering is necessarily part of life, and of loving others. In Christian belief, there would be no redemption without suffering. Good comes from difficulties in surprising ways. But it is good to unite our sufferings with the sufferings of Jesus.
- ☐ Teach your child about how to accept the biggest challenges. A parent's fortitude is crucial in this area. If the opportunity presents itself, show what it means to accompany a dying person, helping them die with love of God.
- ☐ Discuss the benefits of showing lifelong commitment to one's friends.

Does your teen have all the qualities needed for happiness in adult life and relationships? What goals should you set?

[P for C: 137]

Characteristics of Resilient Teenagers

Prioritise

Heart to Heart

The integration of convictions and emotions is the very stuff of virtue. Emotions are our motivators and are vitally important for initial intuitive evaluations of people and situations, for our energetic responses, and for relationships, but if we allow ourselves to be blindly led by emotion, the consequences are terrible...addictions and compulsions, lives filled with chronic anxiety, insensitivity to others and broken relationships, just for starters.

Least-at-risk young persons tend to have the following features. Consider each factor. Discuss what you can both do to assist.	Your teen's current level of development Best > Worst			Action you can take.
Parental connectedness (security, trust, open and straightforward communication, sense of positive regard)				
Connectedness in their peer group				
Connectedness with a mentor: with someone to whom they strongly relate and with whom they can talk trustingly, having 'one caring adult' makes a very significant difference.				
Motivated friendship group				
Sustained application in studies				
Balanced extracurricular interests				
Spiritual and moral values				
Ability to manage emotions				
Ability to set goals for oneself				
Capacity for problem solving				
Generous orientation to others				
Capacity to seek advice				
Degree of comfort to be in the real world and in spending time with others. Avoidance of excessive screen time.				
Home life free of discord				
Assertive confidence to address challenging people or issues.				

[P for C: 145]

The Great Wall of China

Learning from others

'...parents ensure the prudent use of the media by training the conscience of their children....'
Pope Benedict XVI

The journey to self mastery requires young people to put their own boundaries.

Expo Mejia, teacher and rugby coach, talks to teens about how, right through their childhood, their parents have put the Great Wall of China around them but now it is up to them. They put their own 'Great Wall of China', keeping out of their lives what is evil, false and half true, whatever is ugly and angry.

The things we love are the very passports to our souls ... so we all have to be very discerning about what we love. Seneca, Nero's tutor, saw the evils that captured the mind of his pupil. He urged *'Associate with people who are likely to improve you'* and he warned of the dangers of entertainments:

> *'You ask me to say what you should avoid. My answer is this: the mass crowd.... I never come back home (from the gladiatorial shows) with quite the same moral character... it is through the medium of entertainment, that vices creep into one with more than usual ease.... I go home more selfish, more self seeking, more self indulgent. Yes, and what is more, a person crueller and less humane.'*

If the entertainments and the peer group of choice of your teenager do not share your values you will find yourself undermined. This is true for school, sports teams, sleep overs and *Snapchat*.

And when young people are in a crowd that scorns sincerity and generosity they are already in dangerous territory. A parent's constant loving words and presence can make all the difference for them. Others, less fortunate, can seem unreachable.

1. What challenges do today's teens face that their parents never had to face?
2. What values that you are not totally happy with are impacting on your child?
3. What is a practical affectionate way of dealing with this?
4. What challenges can you foresee in the coming years? What can you do now to forestall a later problem?
5. What challenges do dads experience in trying to establish a close relationship with a boy in early teens? What are some of the solutions?
6. What are the new challenges that mums face once kids enter teenage years?

[P for C: 68]

Legal Does Not Equal Moral

Parent-child talk

'Being pure in spirit and pure in heart might not win you a lot of money but will give you something even more precious, peace of heart.'
Dr Takashi Nagai to his children

Psychiatrist and holocaust survivor Victor Frankl, in *The Unconscious God*, held that a partner cannot be a means to an end, and that a sexual relationship requires permanent monogamous commitment. Anything else would be less than human. Theology of the Body adds that sexual relations ought be open to life if true love is, in fact, the gift of oneself.

Yet civil marriage laws hold that marriages need not be life long, and that sexual relations between consenting adults are acceptable. Homosexuality and same sex marriage are legal. Pornography and sexual self-indulgence are endemic in our culture.

How can we deal with these issues in discussions with teenagers, educating but not coercing them? Forming their minds and convictions without diminishing their freedom? It can help to distinguish what is legal from what is moral, with moral understood in the classical sense as what is good for me as a human being.

For example, to hold Marxist views is legal, but anyone who knows the track record of Mao, or Stalin, or Che Guevara, or Pol Pot, could never recommend Marxism. Smoking is legal but why would anyone positively recommend to a young person that they take up smoking? To do so, given the documented health impacts, would be terrible parenting. Same sex marriage may be legal in some jurisdictions but that does not mean that parents should not warn their children against active homosexuality.

Education is needed. Give the facts. Active homosexuality brings serious health risks, reduced life expectancy as demonstrated in large random sexuality surveys, an arguably unfulfilling lifestyle and even higher suicide rates. Give the facts about same sex attraction and gender dysphoria, that neither are wholly attributable to genes. Identical twin studies show this. For example, one Australian study published in 2000 found that if one twin identifies as gay, only about one in nine genetically identical siblings will also identify as gay. There is no gay gene.

It is not a question of vilifying anybody, but of the parents' right to teach their own values to their own children. Just because something is legal does not mean it is good. Truth is powerful.

1. Discuss how you can best explain to your child the vital distinction between legal and moral *before* it becomes an emotional issue.

[P for C: 138]

Putting the Case

'To be a man is, precisely, to be responsible. It is to know shame at the sight of poverty which is not of our making.'
Antoine de Sainte-Exupéry

Read the following episode in the life of a university student and discuss the questions that follow.

> One afternoon after his lectures a young law student wandered into a city bookshop and found a book launch about to start. Delighted, he helped himself to the finger food. When an organiser headed towards him with the guest list, he filled his mouth with food to avoid an awkward conversation. Long story short, he ended up sitting through the subsequent speeches and discovered that the main speaker was a prominent high court personality launching a study of homosexual sociology. Unknowingly he had gatecrashed a LGBT book launch. The speaker offered savage criticism of Catholic sexual teaching. Undeterred, the young man put up his hand and said directly, 'I feel you have misrepresented the position of the Catholic Church on sex'. The speaker rebuffed him, but the student held his ground. A lively to and fro ensued. Later the speaker complimented him and gave him his card.

1. What is the best way to present a positive view of marriage to your teenager?

2. What is the best way for you to educate against behaviours and ideologies that clash with your family's values?

[P for C: 154]

Where Are Your Fathers?

Case study

'Mothers who clearly communicate to their teens that they disapprove of early sex have kids who delay sexual involvement. Fathers who convey that message and are emotionally close to their children have the same effect.'
Thomas Lickona

> Driving through the cinema district of the city on one Friday evening Bob stopped at traffic lights. Fourteen- and fifteen-year-old girls, heavily made up and dressed accordingly, were playing up to the boys outside a hotel. The boys needed little encouragement and were all over them. As Bob watched this he was thinking, 'Where are your fathers? Do they love you this little?'

1. STDs are widespread in teenage and young adult populations. Multiple sexual partners drop the probabilities for a later lifelong partnership. Worst of all, children led into promiscuous behaviours miss out totally on the spiritual joy for which purity is a prerequisite. And whose fault is so much of this? Jim Stenson describes fathers as 'family protectors' and Meg Meeker writes of the need for fathers to defend their daughters. Psychologist Tom Lickona writes bluntly of lasting damage that accrues from juvenile sexual encounters and of the duty of parents to be ahead of the wave. Why are so many parents not in the game?

2. Sometimes teenagers are more open with Snapchat friends than with their own parents. What causes this distance?

3. How can parents ensure they are close enough to their teenagers to offer life-guidance?

[P for C: 151]

Think Through These Questions

'There is no fruit that is not bitter before it is ripe.'
Pubilius Syrus

Are you building these strong convictions in your teenage son or daughter?

- Purity is for all of us, adults and children. Self-dominion and integrity in life are keys to true love.
- The sexual relationship of a man and woman committed to each other for life is a great gift, a great source of unity of hearts and minds, and a beautiful sharing in God's creative power.
- Happiness is the result of generosity not selfishness.
- A sexual relationship is psychologically bonding. Transient intimate relationships cause great harm to ourselves and others by the psychological and moral baggage they create.
- Sexual relationships that deliberately avoid life are already a pact with selfishness and contradict the idea of love as self-giving.
- In pornography, contraception, and same sex relationships, society presents sex as individualistic gratification. The true meaning of marriage has been lost or forgotten by many, and this brings great unhappiness into the lives of so many.
- A child is always a blessing, but it is a terrible injustice to the child to bring that child into the world without a stable loving home and parents who are committed to each other for life. Therefore, it is wrong to enter into a sexual relationship without having promised fidelity for one's life. Premarital sex ignores the rights of a possible child and is a deep lack of respect particularly for the girl who could be left with the child.
- The promises of marriage before God protect the rights of the partner and children.
- Friendships between teenage boys and girls require sensible guidelines. Frequent meeting, physical contact and personal encounters require prudent parameters. We need to understand how easily influenced we can be by our peers in certain situations, and how certain uninhibited social venues and behaviours make it much harder for a person to maintain self-possession. We need to avoid difficult situations before we become immersed in them.
- Excessive alcohol consumption, or use of any drugs such as marijuana, ecstasy, and amphetamines will lead to serious problems.

What can you improve?

_____
_____
_____

[P for C: 137]

Use Technology to do Good

Take the test

Technology is marvellous, but it also comes with the power to marginalize parents and to deliver heavy baggage if we are not discriminating consumers. For some young people it is all-consuming and when that happens, parents are no longer in the game! They are no longer the decisive factor in a child's upbringing. Every parent needs to have a game plan.

Rate your current approach out of 10 for each.

____ Put your best creativity into creating family life. Fight the trend towards profound individualism. Use technology to improve communication, to build extended family, but never to undermine family relationships.

____ Ensure people are more important than things. Be utterly realistic in your own use of technology. Real company is better than virtual company. Those with us deserve our full attention.

____ Establish customs of close communication based on affection.   You cannot force your way into a teenager's world... they must open their hearts and minds to you. Remember you are educating to build convictions, not gain conformity with rules. Don't spy on your teenager's use of technology ... open conversations and trust are essential.

____ Know the facts because your son or daughter tells you: what they are doing online, how they are spending their time, who they are with (even virtually), what influences are coming into their lives (especially via social media). Parents oblivious to these deeply influential players in the lives of their children are marginalized.

____ Be authentic. Social media lends itself to anonymous contributions ... somehow creating the illusion that we need not be responsible for our own actions or words. Talk deeply about truth and sincerity with ourselves and with others. Speak of some of your own life experiences in this regard. Discuss where these qualities are present, and absent in the digital world.

____ Talk about how you manage your time and why you do so. Discuss how technology can save time. Talk about time as a great gift that can be used well or squandered.

____ Share your experience. Explain that digital wisdom and digital self-control are virtues for all of us, adults and children and that digital technology by its repetitive nature is very habit forming..

____ Promote positive content above the trivial and superficial, and less appropriate content. Speak your mind about shameful material. Be clear, calm and straightforward about what you approve and disapprove of. Every choice online improves us or diminishes us.

____ Keep yourself free from creating 'needs' for ourselves... a newer iPhone, a must have app. Just something is affordable doesn't mean it is needed.

____ Talk as a couple about your family culture. Bind yourself to the guidelines. Talk one on one with each child to launch the project. Hold a family meeting regularly to review the guidelines.

Total _____

A score of >80 suggests you are keeping it positive, and therefore you are connecting.

[P for C: 117, 148]

Be Informed

Learning from others

'The research shows that by deliberately conditioning our brain, we might be able to control habits, good and bad.'
Anne Graybiel and Kyle Smith, Scientific American

- Come up to speed. Share your teenager's fascination with all that is good in cyber technology.
- Read up on research into the three principal effects of screen violence on viewers: short term aggression, desensitisation, and a certain paranoia, seeing threats where there are no threats.
- Talk about how willpower is built, for example by reading Angela Duckworth's *Grit*. Talk about how willpower is developed across many associated areas... getting up on time, not complaining, studying hard, etc.
- Read an article about internet and gaming addiction and talk about what you have learned from it.
- Read Thomas Lickona's *How to Raise Kind Kids* and talk about the lessons you take from it about loving respect for others as a crucial value in life.
- Read *Scientific American*, 'Good habits, Bad habits'. Talk together as a couple about the implications. Share your discussions in a positive way in parent child talks.
- Read up on the growing field of Internet gaming disorder and ask your teen how his or her friends are coping. There are nine symptoms proposed by DSM-5, (Diagnostic and Statistical Manual of Mental Disorders - the diagnostic tool published by the American Psychiatric Association) to diagnose Internet gaming disorder. Five or more of these symptoms are required for a diagnosis.

    1. preoccupation (spent too much time thinking about games)
    2. withdrawal (felt moody or anxious when unable to play)
    3. tolerance (increased playtime to keep excitement high)
    4. inability to reduce playing (felt that I should play less but could not)
    5. give up other activities (reduced or lost interest in other activities)
    6. continue despite problems (kept playing even though it caused problems)
    7. deceive (keep others from knowing how much I play)
    8. escape mood (played to escape uncomfortable feelings)
    9. and risk (risked friends or opportunities due to games)

[P for C: 147]

Movie Nights with an Emerging Adult

Family activity — Family Meeting

> *'Not everybody can be famous. But everybody can be great, because greatness is determined by service.'*
> **Martin Luther King, Jr**

Here are some discussion themes following family movie nights.

Present the truth. Have a light touch. Don't get in an argument. Truth has its own power.

Some suggested movies listed under each in brackets.... but you can take this approach with a great range of movies.

1. Marriage and family. Friendships. Love as gift of self. Justice. (*The Family Man, Unplanned, The Lady, Bella*... what further titles can you add?)
   - *'Man can only truly discover himself through a sincere gift of himself.'* - Vatican II
     Dedicated to the care of others.
   - Easy to live with. Manages feelings and temperament out of love for others.
   - *'If you see a need, act.'* - St Mary of the Cross
     Quick to serve. Strives against self-centredness, focusing attention on ourselves, posting up photos of myself, etc.
   - Kindness, courtesy, gratitude, optimism, order and cheerfulness are ways of serving others.
   - Loyalty. Pay attention. Remember birthdays. Send thank you notes.
   - Openness. We are open with each other in a family. *'A problem shared is a problem halved.'*
   - We open our home. We like to make friends. Friendships bring new experiences and commitments.
   - *'Make me a channel of your peace.'* -St Francis. Be an instrument for Our Lord to touchthe hearts of family and friends.
   - We can never do enough to look after mum.

2. Work. Fortitude. (*Cry Freedom, Biko, All the Kings Men, Twelve Years a slave, Unbroken, Apollo 13*... what further titles can you add?)
   - I look on my work as service, and as preparing myself to serve others.
   - Perseverance. I cannot be happy with second rate jobs. Attention to detail. Personal timetable.
   - I accept responsibility for mistakes, and I learn from them.
   - The great task of Christians through their work is to *'order society according to God's plan'*- Vatican II
   - Unity of life. *'One of the gravest errors of our time is the gap between the faith which many profess and the practice of their daily lives.'* – St John Paul II
   - Professional ambition is a good thing... not for my glory, but to do good for others by being the best at what I do. I attach myself to the best teachers I can. I have big ideals and dreams.
   - Fulfilment of our ordinary duties is our path to sanctity.

3. Personal integrity. Self-control. (*Ben Hur, Babette's Feast, Grand Torino, Hacksaw Ridge, The Hurt Locker*... what further titles can you add?)
   - *'Blessed are the pure of heart. They shall see God.'* We need a pure heart if we are to be able to focus on God and others. Impurity develops habits of deep self-centredness.
   - Pornography degrades women and ruins future relationships.
   - God has a plan for each of us. Pray every day to discover that plan.
   - For most, that plan is marriage. Prepare to give yourself to the girl of your dreams by living holy purity with great refinement.
   - Have a daily devotion to Our Lady. In the Rosary I entrust myself and those I love to Our Lady.
   - Give leadership. Talk to your friends if you see they are making bad decisions.
   - Leave 'going steady' until the time comes to think about the girl you will marry. Build friendships but don't give your heart yet.
   - It is very easy to fall into the traps of promiscuity and cohabitation. Help your friends. Don't judge.
   - We manage technology. It doesn't manage us.

4. Faith. Love for truth. (*Molokai, Risen, Frost Nixon, Pawn Sacrifice, Amistad, Chosen, Greater Glory, 12 Angry men, Fr Stu*... what further titles can you add?)
   - We must rediscover *'appreciation of the life of grace.'* - St John Paul II
   - Love the sacraments. *'We draw our strength from the Eucharist.'* - St John Paul II
   - Be sincere. Avoid occasions of sin. Never be scared of opening your heart in confession.
   - Pray daily. Schedule it or it won't happen. *'In prayer we give ourselves back to God.'* - Benedict XVI
   - *'The ordinary way for men to be saved is through the help of other men. A spiritual guide is needed for seeking sanctity.'* - Leo XIII
   - *'By its very nature, the Christian vocation is also a vocation to the apostolate.'* - Vatican II

[P for C: 128]

Changing Your Own Parenting Behaviours

Parent-child talk

> *'The greatest gift a parent can give a child is the determination to improve oneself.'*
> **James Stenson**

Use these strategies to bring about changes in your habitual approaches, or to coach an older child to take responsibility for his or her own goal setting.

- Sincere acknowledgement of mistakes.
- Cultivate reflective sorrow for behaviours that have, intentionally or unintentionally, impacted on others – remember that emotion, including negative emotions of sorrow and shame, can be powerful motivators to future action or change.
- Specify concrete actions for which you wish to build a habit thereby overlaying old habits with new preferred behaviours: getting up on time, eating the right foods, carrying out acts of service to others, smiling when tired, etc.
- Be realistic. Do whatever you need to do to reinforce the new behaviour (eg very specific commitment, a structured anger management programs, a plan for regular review with someone else).
- Establish reminders and triggers that keep the goal in front of you.
- Be joyful. Keep present the benefits to others that will come with mastery of the changed behaviour.
- Now for repetition and guided practice. Stay at it.
- Readiness to accept the support of others, including one's spouse, in order to change one's behaviour.
- Patience and perseverance.

Now apply these principles to a specific goal.

Be specific about the issue you want to address?	Visualise the negatives of this behaviour. Think particularly of the direct or indirect harm to others.	Specify the new behaviour that you want to consolidate.	Decide if you will have an accountability partner. Who? How often will you talk?	How else will you reinforce the new behaviour until it becomes second nature?

[P for C: 34]

APPENDICES

Teaching Temperance

Temperance refers to habits of self-control whereby we develop a facility to moderate impulsive desires by deliberate choices of what we know to be good for us. In its complete development, temperance refers to the joy that we find in persons, activities and things that are truly for our benefit. This virtue empowers us to reason clearly and love wisely, because our choices are no longer subject to thoughtless impulses.

Core parenting approaches:
- **Sound emotional example, by finding joy in the right things**, is the key to teaching temperance. Our goal is to raise children with a great love and desire for what is good, true and beautiful. Emotion is the great motivator in our lives, and temperance means well calibrated emotional responses so that we are attracted to the good, the true and the beautiful. First comes God, then people, and then things.
- **Refined reward expectations** are at the heart of temperance. These conditionings are established by repeated guided experiences and by emotional example. Let us help children not get into the habit of raiding the fridge, putting fun over duty to others, keeping others waiting at the table because they didn't stop playing.
- **Obedience** is a key to learning temperance. Teaching temperance is first of all a matter of training impulsive attractions to enjoyable things, by guiding children in the direction of positive repeated experiences. Children learn to subject their impulsive desires to the reasoned directions of the parent. 'By obeying a parent's reason, children learn to later obey their own,' is Aristotle's dictum.
- **Anger management is crucial**. Ultimately a problem with anger management is a learned impulsive response to which a child has become conditioned. It may be an inability to manage one's fears at not being in control, or it may simply be an imitative behaviour learned as a child that we never overcame. Regardless, if we lose our temper with any sort of regularity, it means that we place our own emotional indulgence over the distress we cause in others.
- **Mindfulness of where one's attention is going** is an important skill in life. Where our attention goes, our thoughts and desires go; temperance means developing habitual self-control of what we pay attention to.
- **Order and simple timetables** build a culture of positive repeated experiences and help a child build habits of eating and playing with moderation, so they have reasonable boundaries and do not dominate in a person's life.
- **Purity and modesty** are best taught through a culture that honours the right to privacy and the right to personal intimacy.

Hence:
- **Give careful emotional example**, showing a child, by your delight and joy, what is lovable and good for us, and by your sadness and aversion, what should be avoided and is bad for us.
- Keep the emphasis on **finding joy in good things** rather emphasising the negative and finding fault.
- **Manage the inputs** that a child receives, conscious of the power of first experience and also of the conditioning power of repeated experiences.
- **Establish predictable routines**.
- **Teach that people are always more important than things**.

- **Give reasons. You are raising a child to run their own life**. Teach a simple understanding of temperance. Teach a child to differentiate between thoughtless curiosity and a choice to pay attention. Teach discrimination between things that are always good (caring for someone in need), things that need moderation (eating and playing), and things that are never good (lying, etc).

Priorities for religious education:

- We love God by our **kindness and attention to others**.
- Show **wonder and joy in the face of the natural world and creation**.
- **Put prayer first and in the best place** in your day. **Show the joy it gives you, and reinforce with your explanations**.
- **Show that your habits of sacraments give you great happiness**.
- **Teach purity explicitly**: that our bodies temples of the Holy Spirit, and that we honour God when we honour his temple.

Points to think about.

Do I make deliberate choices of what I pay attention to, of what I put time into? How well do I manage my thoughts: 'Whatever is true, whatever is honourable, whatever is just, whatever is pure, whatever is lovely, whatever is gracious, if there is any excellence, if there is anything worthy of praise, think about these things (Phil 4:8).' Do I seek what is good, noble and beautiful, shunning cheap imitations? Can I easily say 'no' to myself? Do I remake any habits of pampering myself and overeating; do I set small, practical, daily goals? Do I offer others only positive emotions, affection and kindness? Do I overcome the impulse to return negative emotion to those who show me negative emotion? Do I establish a positive emotional tone in my family by my cheerful face?

Teaching Fortitude

Fortitude refers to the positive conditionings that we have established in our character in the face of pain and discomfort. No longer do we either want to avoid discomfort at all costs, or become discouraged, or put up with difficulties for merely self-indulgent honours, power or wealth. Rather we develop the habit of putting up with difficulties, even serious difficulties, for truly worthy and noble goals. Fortitude empowers us to love God and others.

Core parenting approaches:

- **Refined habits of enduring pain, difficulties and discomfort** for a good reason are at the heart of temperance. We develop these conditionings by repeated experiences and emotional example, and by the conviction that there are priorities that must take precedence over comfort..
- As for temperance, **obedience is a key** to the development of fortitude in a small child.
- **Demand always with affection and have expectations**. Help children understand that you want what is best for them.
- **Have a simple daily family timetable**.
- **Small duties, simple rules in the home, and daily routines** such as getting up on time, if carried out consistently and monitored by parents, build resilience in the face of difficulty.
- **Calm correction from parents** that helps a child look forward, set realistic goals, and take ownership is a necessary approach. These approaches are in contrast to correction that dwells on the fault and seems to dwell on the failure.
- **Teach that feelings may not be a good guide**. At times we need to give ourselves reasons to do things we know are important even if the feelings are initially not there.
- **Teach commitments and promises as** a way of holding ourselves to convictions.
- **Create family culture**: work before play, we clean up after ourselves, we get up when we are called, we don't complain, we don't put things off out of laziness, we only need to ask once, we all chip in, we put things back where they belong, mum doesn't do anything someone else can do, etc.
- **Insist on 'having another go', 'trying again'**. Help your child see that we need a mindset that does not give up easily.
- **Celebrate the small victories** that result from perseverance.

Hence:

- **Insist calmly and persistently on obedience** to reasonable requests.
- **Be predictable**… in your emotional reactions, and in the consequences that follow misbehaviour.
- **Be optimistic**, showing how to break a difficult goal down into doable chunks.
- **Show that work gives you great joy. It is a school of service to others and fortitude.**
- **Show that difficult challenges don't take away your joy**: attending to a sick child in the middle of the night, putting up with an unexpected breakage, etc.
- **Take on physically challenging recreations** with the family… bike riding, bushwalking, etc.
- Don't complain, but do always **help your child to open up their heart** something is difficult for them. There is a big difference.

Priorities for religious education:

- **Teach that God comes first** in our lives by daily gratitude, habits of prayer, visiting the Blessed Sacrament, and regular confession.
- **Let children see your joy** at prayer, and at receiving the Blessed Sacrament and getting to confession.
- **Give leadership** in family piety.
- Build family culture. We don't leave out our **daily family prayers**. We say the family rosary, and even small children stay for one mystery.
- **We honour God by living with the naturalness of a Christian family**. If that means others know that we pray before meals and don't watch certain movies, that's fine. We don't over indulge ourselves. People are more important than products. Helping someone who is busy is more important than resting ourselves.
- **We don't dodge the hard conversations** when something needs to be clearly but courteously corrected.

Points to think about.

Do I see work as a school of fortitude? Can I say 'yes' to noble challenges? Am I reliable in the jobs I am responsible for? Do I clean up after myself? Am I orderly? Do I stay calm in the face of difficulties? Am I a cheerful person despite difficulties? Can I follow a timetable? Am I optimistic and encouraging of others? Do I face and overcome my fears: of discomfort, of embarrassment, of loneliness, of unpopularity, of having hard conversations? Do I dodge physical exertion? Do I have another go after failures never giving up? Do I make and honour commitments? Do I articulate my convictions? Do I give leadership, shunning the comfort of waiting for someone else to lead.

Teaching Justice

Justice refers to the habitual choices of empathy, care and respect we show towards others in our words and actions, and to our habit of choosing to fulfil of our duties to others. Because it is the virtue of the will, or the power that we have of choosing and loving, justice is the habit of loving wisely, of putting people above things, and duties to others above our own pleasures.

The alternatives to justice are an habitual self-centredness manifested in our choices, or an inability to act at all.

Justice is the foundation virtue for Charity in the spiritual domain. Both are directed to others: Justice to our natural duties to others, and through Charity, God's own love in which we share in Baptism, we put God first in our lives, as the gift of Faith calls us to do. Jesus himself points out the profound link between doing things for others and doing things for God: 'as often as you do this for least of your brethren you do it to Me.' Ultimately, the habit of religious practice, is a duty of justice towards God who has given us so much.

Core parenting approaches:
- **See family as the natural place to do things for others out of love**, without expecting a reward. Build this culture in every dimension of family life. This is the first lesson in love of God.
- **A culture of generosity is necessary in the home**... especially in constant deeds of service to family members, in understanding the needs of each other, and attending to them promptly.
- **Attention to each other is essential**. Important too are small details of kindness, common courtesies, habits of listening and of not wanting to be the centre of attention.
- **We must strive to be easy to live with**, managing our emotions with self control, but putting our passionate efforts into helping others.
- **Gratitude should be a constant feature of family life**.
- **Members of a family keep their word to each other**.
- **Habits of solidarity with those in need bring joy into family life**.

Hence:
- **The primary task of a parent is to teach their children to love**: to be capable of loving with all their heart, soul, mind and strength.
- **Parents must make of their home a school of love**.
- **Parents' example of love for each other is decisive** in showing the priority that we must give to others in our lives.
- Parents must show that **love never runs out**.
- **We take full responsibility for forming the character of our children**.
- Parents need to show constantly the **joy that comes from helping others**: lighting up when we see each other, joy in serving a neighbour, etc.

With respect to religious education the key priorities would be:

- **Jesus is our model of love**. He gives us example of how we should love: giving our very lives for others as he gave his. For most of us this comes down to constant small choices. We need to teach children to have this lively daily struggle.
- **Let us strive to be Christ to others**, and teach children to do likewise.
- **Let us talk to Jesus in prayer as our greatest friend**, and teach children to do likewise.
- **Let us offer our work well done**. In this we imitate Jesus in his desire to obey the will of the Father and give glory to the Father.
- **Love is in the daily detail or else it is absent**. We should raise children to be deeply aware that Jesus asks us into a personal relationship of love. We should respond in daily details of gratitude, trust and contrition at offending him.
- **St Paul urges us 'have the same mind as Christ Jesus'**. To love as Jesus loves, we need to love others without exception, to delight in what gives him joy, and grieve in what gives him sorrow. Let us look at all others with the eyes of Our Lord, being deeply kind and attentive to each person we encounter in the day. Let us also make many acts of reparation for our own sins and the offenses to God around us.

Points to think about.

Am I a kind person? Do I treat others well habitually? Do I suffer when those around me suffer? Do I share their joys and sorrows? Am I habitually courteous and punctual? Do I know how to apologise? Do I know how to forgive? Am I first in acts of service? Do I give in to impatience and anger? Do I make service the lynchpin of family life? Do I drop what I am doing to give my full attention to others? Do I ever think critically of others, or do I correct the behaviour finding excuses for the person: 'Think others as being better than yourself (Phil 2:3).' Am I a grateful person? Do I serve those who are less fortunate?

Teaching Prudence

Prudence bestows self management on the impulsive raw material of which we are made. In each one of our actions, we either act on impulse, or we give ourselves sound objective reasons to act: prudence is the well-established habit of reflecting on reality before acting so that our actions are well informed and good, in other words that they are reasonable and worthy of a human being. The virtue of prudence has two aspects. On the one hand it is the habit of proposing practical and effective goals for action, and on the other it is the habit of judging situations and actions according to reality and to a well formed conscience, according to objective moral norms.

The alternatives to prudence are an inability to recognise truth and a readiness to accept non-reality, sentiment, or opinion as one's basis for action, or an ineptitude for practical steps required to reach a goal.

When the truths of Faith inform the virtue of prudence, supernaturalising it, all our choices are informed with Christian convictions: not least that God in his Providence cares for me at every moment, and that my every choice must give glory to God and manifest my love for him.

Core parenting approaches:
- **We are not the centre of the universe**. I strive to fill my life and my thoughts with my family and friends, and the needs of my neighbours. I don't focus my attention on myself.
- **I listen to my spouse**. We are a team and stronger because we have different points of view and work together.
- **I listen to my children, and explain to them what is right and wrong, and why**. I realise that the aim of raising a child is not to obtain conformity with my expectations, but to foster sound personal convictions in the child.
- **I encourage my children to set goals**.
- **I help children break big tasks down** so they can practically resolve them.

Hence:
- **I foster sincerity**. I make it easy for my child to speak to me. I give daily 1:1 time to each child.
- **I help my children learn to prioritise their tasks**. Working on paper can help.
- **I create opportunities for my child to make decisions and set goals** and support him or her in achieving these.
- **I correct my child with affection** whenever there is a need, and then I follow up progress as often as needed.
- **We hold family meetings** so that children are consulted and gain practice in thinking about issues.
- **I help my child never to hide behind excuses**.
- **As parents we have established some goals** to improve our parenting and the culture in the home.

With respect to religious education key priorities would be:

- **I am convinced that without sacraments we lack strength to live according to our Faith**.
- **I am convinced that the more we know, the more we can love**. Therefore I strive to grow in my knowledge of my Faith. I read the scriptures daily. I listen to podcasts. I encourage my child in this area also.
- **I strive to build a contemplative spirit in my own character**. I set aside time for prayer each day and coach my teenage children to do likewise.
- **Self knowledge is an important prerequisite for self improvement**. I develop the habit of a daily examination of conscience at the end of the day, and encourage my child to do the same.
- **I ask advice and I encourage my children to ask advice** from the priest in confession to obtain well formed consciences.
- **I understand the importance of a daily plan** and the importance of scheduling prayer and other spiritual activities in the day. I lead by example and help my children learn to do this also.

Points to think about.

Do I set goals, priorities and make resolutions? Do I ask advice to find out what is right and true? Do I tell the truth without compromise? Do I avoid excuses? Do I avoid talking about myself or drawing attention to myself. Do I take conversation with others seriously, seeking to learn from others? Do I listen more than I talk? Do I offer gratuitous opinions? Do I think before acting, avoiding impulsive purchases and responses to others? Do I listen to my conscience? Have I problem solving strategies: break challenges down into parts; set interim goals, etc? Do I take time for reflection; do I seek out nature? Do I examine my behaviour daily?

www.ingramcontent.com/pod-product-compliance
Lightning Source LLC
Chambersburg PA
CBHW081919090526
44591CB00015B/2400